EATING OIL
ENERGY USE IN
FOOD PRODUCTION

And God said, Behold, I have given you every herb bearing seed, which is upon the face of all the earth, and every tree, in the which is the fruit of a tree yielding seed; to you it shall be for meat.

—Genesis 1:29

A full belly is a great thing; all else is luxury.

—Lin Yutang

EATING OIL
ENERGY USE IN FOOD PRODUCTION

Maurice B. Green

Westview Press / Boulder, Colorado

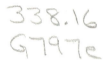

Copyright © 1978 by Westview Press, Inc.

Published in 1978 in the United States of America by
Westview Press, Inc.
5500 Central Avenue
Boulder, Colorado 80301
Frederick A. Praeger, Publisher and Editorial Director

Library of Congress Cataloging in Publication Data
Green, Maurice Berkeley.
    Eating oil.
    Bibliography: p.
    Includes index.
    1. Food industry and trade—Energy consumption. 2. Agriculture—Energy consumption. I. Title.
TP370.5.G73   338.1'6   77-21577
ISBN 0-89158-244-4

Printed and bound in the United States of America

To Catherine

my constant source of energy and inspiration

Contents

Tables

Figures

Photographs

Preface

There are 4,000 million people in the world, of whom 1,000 million are undernourished. However, the 205 million people in the United States, and the people in most other developed countries, enjoy an adequate diet of wholesome and nourishing food, with a great variety of choice, and have to spend only about 20 percent of their disposable incomes to do so. This is possible only because large amounts of fossil fuel energy such as oil are put, on an ever-increasing scale, into the food production, processing, distribution, and preparation systems of their nations. But, as populations increase and the amounts of arable land available remain the same, the law of diminishing returns applies. World resources of fossil fuels are limited and irreplaceable, so their use to bolster food production cannot be continued indefinitely. We cannot go on eating oil for very much longer. The United States, despite its wealth, is not immune from the hunger of the Third World—it is only a matter of time.

This book is addressed to all those who care whether their great-grandchildren will have enough to eat when they are adults, and who also, perhaps, have some concern for the human race as a whole. It is intended to provide facts and figures to show how fast fossil fuel energy is being used up in the developed countries, so that the public may appreciate the seriousness of the problem, and to suggest some ways in which economies might be made. In the final chapters, consideration is given to the problems of feeding the population of the developing countries to whom the expedient of using fossil fuel energy to boost food production is not available.

This is a book by an "amateur" who is deeply concerned by the problems both for the developed and developing countries, but who does not pretend to suggest that he could even begin to solve them. They are problems for governments, but governments will act only if the people demand them to do so, and it is hoped that this book will stimulate readers to press for action—and to be willing to foot the bill.

As the food system is very complex, assumptions have to be made to estimate the amounts of fossil fuel energy used in various parts of it. The figures quoted in this book should not, therefore, be regarded as precise. It is, however, believed that they are of the right order and that any errors are not sufficient to invalidate the arguments advanced or conclusions drawn.

I gratefully acknowledge the many publications on which I have drawn as sources of information. Where figures from any of these have been quoted, references are given in the back of the book in the customary manner for scientific publications. The masses of statistics published by departments of the governments of the United States and the United Kingdom and by trade associations have been particularly valuable, as also were those of the Food and Agriculture Organization.

I also wish to thank Rosalind Evans who typed the manuscript from almost illegible handwriting.

The opinions expressed in the book are entirely my own and do not necessarily reflect the views of my employer, Imperial Chemical Industries Limited.

M.B.G.

Notes on Units

Energy

The unit of energy is the joule (J). A megajoule (MJ) is 1 million joules, a gigajoule (GJ) is 1 billion joules, and a megagigajoule (MGJ) is 1 million gigajoules. One thousand kilocalories (commonly called "calories") are about 4 MJ (4.19). One thousand BTU are almost exactly 1 MJ (1.055). One therm is almost exactly 100 MJ (105.5). One kilowatt/hour is about 4 MJ (3.6). One horsepower/hour is about 2½ MJ (2.68). *One GJ is equivalent to about 7 U.K. gallons or about 8 U.S. gallons of diesel fuel.*

Length

About 2½ (2.54) centimetres (cm) is 1 inch.
One metre (m) (0.91) is about 1 yard.
One kilometre (km) is about 3/5 (0.62) mile.

Area

One hectare (ha) is about 2½ acres (2.47).

One square kilometre (km²) is about 2/5 (0.39) square mile.

One square metre (m²) is about 1.2 square yards.

Volume

One litre (l) is about 1/5 (0.22) U.K. gallon or 1/4 (0.26) U.S. gallon.

The word "gallon" in this book is the U.K. gallon.

Weight

One kilogram (kg) is about 2¼ (2.2) pounds (lbs).

One tonne (t) is about 1.1 U.S. tons (1.12) or about 1 U.K. ton (0.98).

Yield

Kilograms per hectare (kg/ha) are almost the same as pounds per acre (lbs/acre). (1 kg/ha = 1.12 lbs/acre.)

EATING OIL
ENERGY USE IN
FOOD PRODUCTION

CHAPTER ONE

The Nature of the Problem

How long can we go on eating oil? Before we try to answer this question, it is desirable to understand how and why we do eat it. If you live in a developed country like the United States or the United Kingdom, every mouthful of food you eat—unless you gather wild berries by the roadside—irrevocably consumes a finite amount of irreplaceable fossil fuel energy. This is because direct energy in the form of tractor fuel and indirect energy in the form of fertilizers are put into the operations of growing plant food and rearing animal food, and because energy is used in processing, distributing, and preparing food. Each of these stages uses some fossil fuel energy, so by the time the food reaches your table it has accumulated a fossil fuel energy "input." (This is different from the energy that your body can get from food by eating it, which is commonly measured by the "calorie content" and which is the energy "output.") We eat oil, therefore, by putting fossil fuel energy into the processes of food production, into the nation's "food system."

Why do we eat oil? Why is it necessary? The natural laws of thermodynamics decree that, to get more metabolically utilizable energy (that is, energy that can actually be used by your body) out of the food production system, you must either put more energy in or use the existing level of energy more efficiently, so as to achieve a better energy output:input ratio. The only sources of energy available to us are the direct energy of the sun, which plants utilize for us by the process of photosynthesis; the muscle power of men and animals, which is derived from the food they eat; and the energy of past sunshine, which is stored in fossil fuels. Wind and water power are indirect forms of solar energy because wind and rain result from temperature differences brought about by the sun. Ultimately, present or past sunshine is our sole source of energy with the exception of nuclear power.

The human body cannot thrive on sun and air alone; it also needs food. The body is, physically, a complicated coke boiler. It gets its energy by "burning" carbon to carbon dioxide, and the biochemistry of its digestive and respiratory systems is designed to turn the energy of this combustion into the metabolically utilizable form of adenosine triphosphate, which is the only fuel that will actually power our muscles. We get the carbon we need from the carbon dioxide in the atmosphere, but we cannot use this directly; it is made available to us only through the mediation of photosynthesis by the plants that provide our food and the food for our animals. Plants, unlike animals, possess the ability to take carbon dioxide from the air and to combine it with water from the soil by the action of sunlight to build the sugars, starches, fats, and proteins that we use for our nutrition. Likewise, we cannot use the carbon in fossil fuels directly for our bodily needs; we cannot actually eat oil. We can use it only to provide energy to increase the amounts of crops produced—that is, to increase the total amount of photosynthesis that determines the total amount of carbon dioxide "fixed" by plants and thus made available for our use as food. We do this by utilizing the fossil fuel energy, directly, in mechanical devices such as tractors or combine harvesters and, indirectly, to manufacture chemicals such as fertilizers and pesticides.

Why do we need to use fossil fuels at all in agriculture? Why cannot we just rely on the energy provided by photosynthesis? Why cannot we, as some people advocate, grow all our food without using manufactured fertilizers or pesticides and by using animal and manpower rather than tractors? The answer is that we could if we were willing to reduce the population of the United States from the 220 million it is today to the 120 million it was in 1930. All that the U.S. government need do is draw up a list of the 100 million inhabitants who are to be allowed to starve and then order most of the remaining population back to work on the land. If the United States used for food production today only the amount of fossil fuel energy that it used in 1930 to feed the population, it would need about 76 million more ha of cropland and about 273 million more ha of farmland than are now being cultivated. This is an increase of about 60 percent over the present amounts of cropland and farmland. These extra amounts are simply not available: practically all land in the United States which can be cultivated is, in fact, being cultivated. Land is not, however, the only consideration. Even if the extra land were available, it would need 20 million agricultural workers—instead of the 4 million currently employed in the U.S.—to achieve 1976 output of food with 1930 input of energy. Similarly, for the United Kingdom to achieve 1976 food production

POPULATION   AND   AGRICULTURAL   WORKERS   IN   U. S.

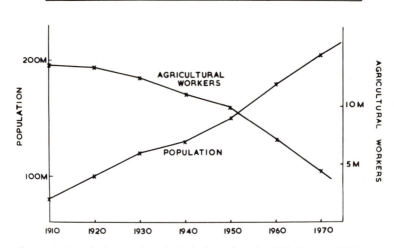

Figure 1. Population and agricultural workers in U.S. *Source:* U.S. government statistics.

with 1930 energy input would require that the amount of arable land now available be approximately doubled and the number of agricultural workers increased approximately fivefold. This is not possible.

The basic reason why we have to use fossil fuels in agriculture should now be quite clear: we have a large and growing population, of which only a small and decreasing percentage are engaged in agricultural production on a limited and dwindling amount of arable land.

Figure 1 shows the upward trend of U.S. population and the downward trend of numbers of U.S. agricultural workers. Figure 2 shows the same thing for the United Kingdom. The total areas of the developed countries such as the United States and United Kingdom are fixed and their amounts of arable land are steadily decreasing as more homes, shopping plazas, freeways, airports, parking lots, etc., are built.

The key factor in the energy in agriculture problem is,

POPULATION AND AGRICULTURAL WORKERS IN U.K.

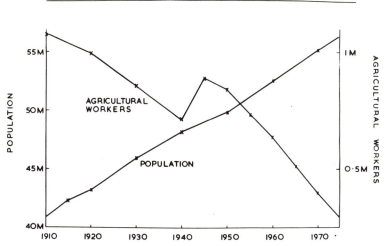

Figure 2. Population and agricultural workers in U.K. *Source:* U.K. government statistics.

therefore, the amount of arable land available per head of population. To understand the problem more clearly, let us consider primitive man. It is commonly believed that he had a hard time, working every minute to scratch together a frugal diet for himself and his family. It is clear that this was not so. The experts who have studied these matters tell us that only a small proportion of primitive man's time was occupied with food gathering and that he had plenty of time to fight the neighbors, sing, dance, make love, draw pictures on the walls of his cave, develop a culture, and use his ingenuity to invent the things which enabled him to progress toward modern civilization. Primitive woman had less time available for such occupations as she was busy bearing and raising children, which is probably why, until recently, most occupations were male-dominated.

Modern studies (Lee 1969) of the Kung bushmen, a primitive tribe still living in Africa, have shown that they

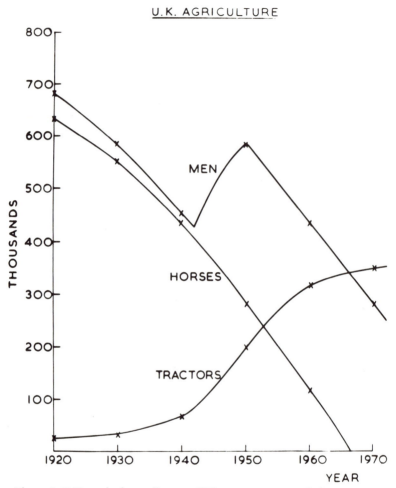

Figure 3. U.K. agriculture. *Source:* U.K. government statistics.

provide themselves with a varied high-protein diet based on nuts, animals, and twenty different types of vegetables by food gathering for 2.5 days out of 7. One day's work by a bushman provides food for himself and three other people. His energy output:input ratio is 7.8 and all the energy he uses is muscle power. But—and this is the key point—he needs

ENERGY INPUT TO U.K. CROP PRODUCTION

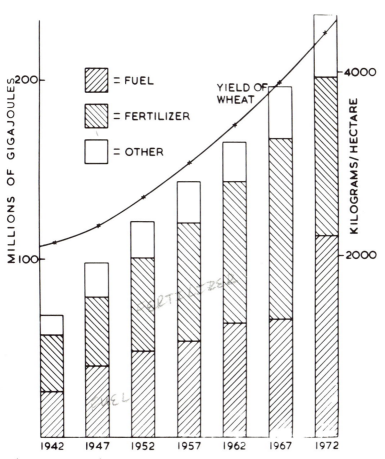

Figure 4. Energy input to U.K. crop production. *Source:* U.K. government statistics.

1,040 ha of land per person to do it. In North America the prairie Indians required 2,500 ha of land per person to meet their food needs, and the arctic Eskimo needed 14,000 ha per person.

By contrast, the present-day U.S. agricultural worker provides in one day's work enough food for himself and sixty other people in the United States and a considerable quantity for export, and he uses only about 2 ha of agricultural land per person to do it. However, his energy output:input ratio is only 0.87, and the major part of the energy input is fossil fuel energy. The British agricultural worker provides in one day's work enough food for himself and fifty-seven other people, and he uses only about 0.35 ha of agricultural land per person to do it, that is, about 1/6 the amount of land per person as in the United States, a reflection of the intensity and efficiency of U.K. agriculture consequent on much higher population density. He pays for this by an energy output:input ratio reduced to 0.34 and, as in the U.S., the major part of the energy input is fossil fuel energy.

So we see the dilemma. For a given input of energy the Kalahari bushman achieves about 9 times as much energy output as the U.S. or twenty-three times as much as the U.K. agricultural worker. But the U.S. agricultural worker produces about 500 times more food per ha than the bushman obtains, and the U.K. agricultural worker produces about 3,000 times more. Low agricultural productivity is energy-efficient; high agricultural productivity is energy-demanding. Given that the populations of the developed countries such as the United States and United Kingdom are going to increase or, at the very least, not substantially decrease, and given that their amounts of arable land and their agricultural labor forces are both limited, then there is no alternative for them. If they are to maintain their present quantity and variety of food and feed their populations adequately, they must put fossil fuel energy into food production. Using such energy to meet the basic human need to eat every day is entirely justified, but the total world resources of fossil fuel are limited. This is why it is imperative to ask the original question, How long can we go on eating oil?

To answer this question it is necessary to know how fast we are using up the available oil so, in subsequent chapters, facts and figures are given to provide this information.

But first let us consider why the farmer was so willing to increase his use of energy. Mechanical equipment such as tractors and combine harvesters are expensive and demand a substantial outlay of capital, and fertilizers and pesticides are not cheap. Yet mechanization has proceeded apace, as shown in figure 3, and the total amount of fossil fuel energy used has accelerated, as shown in figure 4. (These figures are for the United Kingdom but the U.S. picture is similar.) This has cost the farmer a lot of money but he has spent it because it has proved very profitable for him to do so. Although the nation as a whole needs to put fossil fuel energy into agriculture in order to feed an increasing population from a limited amount of land, this is not why farmers did put fossil fuel energy into agriculture. They were motivated not by altruism but by a natural desire to increase their profits and to improve their standard of living.

Consider the direct use of energy—that is, replacement of manpower and horsepower by tractors and other mechanical equipment. The cost of fossil fuel energy to U.S. farms is about $15 per GJ whereas the cost of human energy at $3 per hr is about $6,000 per GJ. The only ways in which it could be made economical for the farmer to go back to manpower would be either to make fossil fuel energy 400 times more expensive, or to reintroduce slavery. A return to horsepower is, likewise, demonstrably uneconomic. In 1940 the amount of cropland needed to feed draft animals in the United States was 16 million ha out of a total cropland of 120 million ha. At this time there were already 1.5 million tractors in use on U.S. farms. Yet to go back even to this degree of mechanization would necessitate reduction of corn

Photo 1A. Old-fashioned farming equipment. (Courtesy of Imperial Chemical Industries Limited.)

production by 35 million t—by about 160 kg for each man, woman, and child in the United States. To do away altogether with mechanization would be clearly out of the question. In the United Kingdom in 1900 1.1 million horses were used on farms and required a total of 1.3 million ha to grow their feed out of a total of 12 million ha of available agricultural land. It is interesting to note that there were 2.4 million horses in the United Kingdom in 1900 used for nonfarm purposes and that these needed another 3 million ha of land to feed them. The horse needs feeding all year round but the tractor needs fuel only when it has a job to do. A farmer cannot nowadays afford to devote 15 percent of his land to feeding horses and it is much more financially rewarding for him to buy a tractor and to increase his income by using the land saved to grow extra

Photo 1B. Modern farming equipment. (Courtesy of Imperial Chemical Industries Limited.)

crops for sale. From a national viewpoint, developed countries such as the United States and United Kingdom need all their land to feed a growing human population and they simply can no longer afford to devote land to feeding horses.

Regarding the financial gain to the farmer of indirect use of fossil fuel energy in fertilizers and pesticides it has been shown that, in Illinois, $1 spent on fertilizers for corn returned $7.23 at 1964 prices, $13.36 at 1971 prices, and $11 at 1976 prices, consequent on increased yields per ha. A survey of tomato production in the United States in 1962 showed that use of fertilizers increased the farmers' gross incomes by 196 percent.

In the United States it has been estimated that each $1 spent on pesticides, provided they are used judiciously and sensibly, produces $4 extra income for the farmer. In the United Kingdom, each £1 spent on pesticides produces £5 extra income. There are a number of examples of studies of the financial returns from pesticide usage on various crops. Use of pesticides on tomatoes in the United States increased the growers' gross incomes by 75 percent. Each $1 spent on pesticides in apple orchards returned $13 in Nova Scotia, $5 in Quebec, and $2.34 in Ontario, and each $1 spent on pesticides for potatoes in Canada returned $6.71. A study of German farms growing cereals and root crops over a 4-yr period showed a gain in crop value of $47.20 per ha for an outlay of $20.30 per ha for pesticides. The estimated increase in value of crops harvested on 10 million ha in Canada treated with herbicides in 1960 at a cost of $8 million was $58 million. Control of stable flies in Illinois dairy barns gave a 7%-30% increase in butterfat production.

It is not easy to produce precise figures for the financial benefits of fertilizers and pesticides for individual crops grown by individual farmers as these vary widely from crop to crop, from farm to farm, and from season to season and depend very much on the skill and economy with which the farmer uses mechanical equipment, fertilizers, and pesticides. The most convincing evidence of the overall financial benefits to the farmers is the fact that in the United States they spent $3 billion on fertilizers and $3.2 billion on pesticides in 1971—which is six times the amount spent in 1966—and farmers do not part with their money easily or for no good reason. They obviously were convinced that the money spent was justified.

The fact that it was so financially rewarding to farmers to put fossil fuel energy into agriculture, either directly or indirectly, has had a profound effect for the nation as a whole on manpower requirements in agriculture, on crop yields per ha, and consequently, on the total amount of food produced. For the first time in history, population has been able to increase while the amount of cultivated land has fallen.

Table 1. The Effect of Fossil Fuel
Energy Input on Output per Man-Hour

Crop	Energy output (in MJ/man-hours)
Rice U.S.	2,800
Corn U.S.	3,800
Cereals U.K.	3,040
Rice tropical peasants	40
Corn tropical peasants	33
Rice tropical subsistence	15
Corn tropical subsistence	28
Peas U.K.	300
Carrots U.K.	150
Brussels sprouts U.K.	45
U.S. or U.K. vegetable garden	4
Bushmen food gatherers	4

Source: Leach 1976.

The effect on manpower is shown by the drop in the number of workers needed in U.S. agriculture from about 12 million in 1930 to about 4 million in 1976, and in U.K. agriculture from about 750,000 in 1930 to about 250,000 in 1976. Herbicides in particular can be used as substitutes for labor. An example of the effects of energy input on manpower requirements for a particular crop is cotton. In 1975 it took 50 man-hours to grow and harvest 1 ha of cotton using chemical weeding and defoliation and mechanical picking, compared with 200 man-hours in 1933 using manual hoeing and picking. Similarly, in 1975 it took

40 man-hours to grow and harvest 1 ha of peanuts, compared with 190 man-hours in 1935, and 22 man-hours to grow and harvest 5000 kg of corn, compared with 135 man-hours in 1945.

Table 2. Increase in Crop Yields in the United States (100 kg/ha)

Crop	1938	1948	1958	1968
Wheat	8.4	11.4	17.4	18.0
Corn	16.3	25.0	30.3	46.1
Cotton	2.6	3.4	5.1	5.6

Source: U.S. government statistics.

The effect of input of fossil fuel energy on output per man-hour is shown in table 1. To facilitate comparisons, the output is given in terms of metabolically utilizable food energy. It will be seen that the output per man-hour in developed countries is by far the greatest in the case of cereal crops. The more specialized vegetable crops, which require more labor, produce less per man-hour. It is interesting to note that the output per man-hour of the citizen of the United Kingdom or United States who grows vegetables in his garden is no better than that of the primitive bushman who gathers food in near desert conditions.

The effects of input of fossil fuel energy on crop yields per ha are indicated by the figures for yield increases shown in tables 2 and 3 for the United States and United Kingdom respectively.

The big upswing dates from 1945, which was the year that mechanization of farming and extensive use of fertilizers and pesticides really got under way. This is shown clearly by figures 5 and 6. The 5-yr moving average for wheat yields in the United Kingdom plotted against the increase in use of

Table 3. Increase in Crop Yields in the United Kingdom (100 kg/ha)

Crop	1915	1925	1935	1945	1950	1955	1960	1965
Wheat	22.0	23.0	23.3	24.0	26.3	33.5	35.8	40.7
Barley	18.0	19.7	21.2	23.9	24.1	32.1	33.0	37.7
Oats	17.7	18.8	20.3	21.7	21.7	26.9	26.6	31.5
Potatoes	158.1	165.7	158.1	180.7	193.3	183.2	218.4	256.0
Sugar beet	..	215.9	228.4	236.0	271.1	308.7	419.2	374.0
Turnips and swedes	358.9	333.8	306.2	379.0	389.0	364.0	484.4	494.5

Source: U.K. government statistics.

direct and indirect fossil fuel energy has already been shown in figure 4. Figure 5 shows particularly dramatically the effect of fossil fuel energy input on crop production during the past 30 yrs.

Of course, some of the yield increases are due to the development of higher-yielding plant varieties, to improved irrigation, and to better cultivation techniques and farm management practices. Nevertheless, fossil fuel energy input is certainly the reason for a very considerable part of these yield increases. It is sometimes possible to analyze the contributions of various inputs. For example, figure 7 shows the average corn yield in Illinois from 1900 to date. Introduction of high-yielding hybrid varieties began in 1935 and was complete by 1940. Fertilizer use increased from 1940 to 1953 but was stable thereafter. From 1953 herbicides and soil insecticides were introduced.

For the consumer, the result of the reduced manpower requirements and increased crop yields has been that, despite population increases, there have in developed countries been adequate supplies of wholesome and nutritious food at

WHEAT IN U.K. SINCE 1100

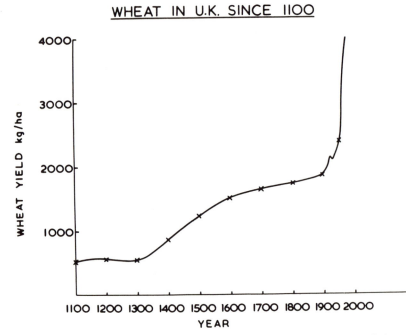

Figure 5. Wheat in U.K. since 1100. *Source:* U.K. government statistics.

reasonable prices. Fewer people have had to work on the land, and the population, on the average, has had to spend a lower proportion of their income on food. This is illustrated in table 4.

Calculations have been made of the economic effects on farmers and on consumers of the withdrawal of some of the current fossil fuel energy inputs from agriculture. It has already been pointed out that to produce 1976 food output in the United States with only the 1930 fossil fuel energy input would require 76 million more ha of cropland and 273 million more ha of farmland, an increase of 60 percent. To have produced the amounts of seventeen crops that were actually produced in 1975 with the yields per ha of 1945 would have required an extra 120 million ha of land—the equivalent of Texas, Arizona, and New Mexico together.

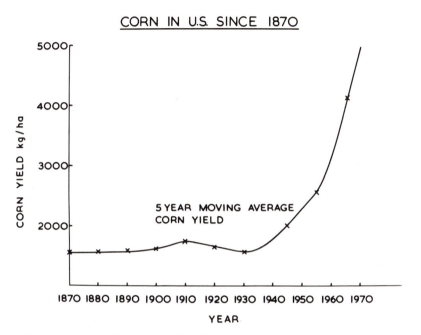

Figure 6. Corn in U.S. since 1870. *Source:* U.S. government statistics.

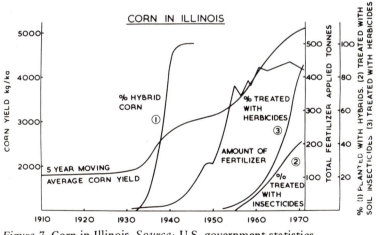

Figure 7. Corn in Illinois. *Source:* U.S. government statistics.

Table 4. The Result of Reduced Manpower
Requirements and Increased Crop Yields

Country	Percentage of laboring population working in agriculture	Average percentage of income spent on food
United States	7	18
Canada	11	21
Australia	11	22
Denmark	17	22
South Africa	30	28
Ireland	35	33
U.S.S.R.	39	56
India	73	66
Nigeria	97	70

Source: FAO statistics.

It has been estimated that, without pesticides and fertilizers, the United States could supply only 40 percent of
the food and fiber needs of its population and would have
nothing available for export. The percentage of their disposable income that individuals would have to spend on
food would rise from 17 percent to 40 percent. Since there
are 25 million people in the United States who have poverty
level incomes, one consequence would be that at least this
25 million, and probably more, would starve. Even if pesticides alone were withdrawn, U.S. production of crops and
livestock would fall by 30 percent and prices would rise by
50%-70%. The U.S. Department of Agriculture has calculated
that withdrawal of the herbicide *2,4-D*, which is used in
wheat production, would add $290 M to production costs
of bread and other wheat products and would necessitate 20
million extra man-hours of work by farmers without any
increase in income. The use of *2,4-D* in wheat has resulted in

enough wheat in 1975 for 130 billion more loaves than in 1940.

That these estimates of the economic effects of withdrawal of energy input are not figments of the imagination is shown by the experience in 1970 when the southern corn leaf blight got out of control and 20 billion kg of corn were lost. Corn prices rose from 5.3c/kg to 6.6c/kg and stayed at this level for a year with a total extra cost to the consumer of $2 billion.

There is, therefore, no doubt that input of fossil fuel energy into agriculture is financially advantageous both for the farmer and for the consumer, and that any substantial reduction in this energy input would have very serious consequences for the well-being and financial situation of the nation and of its inhabitants. Yet supplies of fossil fuel are limited and economies in its use must be made. The facts and figures given in this book on the actual amounts of fossil fuel energy put into the food system of the nation and the amounts of fossil fuel energy used by the nation for other purposes may suggest where the required economies can best be made.

CHAPTER TWO

Energy in Primary Agricultural Production

Energy is used whenever material is processed or transported; thus, at each stage of its manufacture, a commodity acquires an energy input that is carried on to the next stage. The final product has cumulative indirect energy inputs from the intrinsic energies of all the materials derived from fossil fuels which were used in its manufacture, as well as direct energy inputs from the heat and electricity used in its processing.

Computer programs have been developed which calculate and sum up all these energy inputs for a specified chemical product such as a fertilizer or pesticide. These take into account all ancillary energy inputs as well as the main energy inputs, such as the energy that goes into building and maintaining the manufacturing plant and equipment, feeding and transporting the workers, disposing of effluents, and all other operations which utilize energy. They also take into account all energy needed to produce the coal, oil, natural gas, and electricity that are used either as sources of raw materials or to provide energy for processing. Thus, all energy inputs of all kinds are "rolled back" to a fossil fuel equivalent.

The energy figures given in this book are, in accordance with modern practice, given in SI units. For those who are not accustomed to thinking in such units, one gigajoule (GJ) of energy is about equivalent to 7 U.K. gal (8 U.S. gal) of diesel fuel, and a megajoule (MJ) is one-thousandth of this.

Table 5. Energy Inputs for
Various Fertilizers (GJ/t)

Nitram	25.4
Urea	34.7
ICI 9 (9.25.25)	13.7
ICI 1 (15.15.21)	16.2
ICI 5 (17.17.17)	17.5
ICI 2 (22.11.11)	19.7

Source: I.C.I. 1974.

Table 6. Energy Inputs for
Elemental Constituents of
Fertilizers (GJ/t)

Nitrogen	81.2
Phosphorus pentoxide	13.8
Potassium oxide	8.0
Coal	25.0

Source: I.C.I. 1974.

Table 5 shows the total energy inputs for a number of fertilizers and table 6 shows the energy inputs for the individual fertilizer constituents, nitrogen, phosphorus, and potassium, compared with the intrinsic energy of coal. Packaging of the fertilizer into polyethylene bags adds about 1 GJ/t, and transport and delivery to the farmer add about 0.3 GJ/t.

Table 7. Energy Inputs for Various Pesticides (GJ/t)

Herbicides		Fungicides		Insecticides	
MCPA	130	Ferbam	61	Methyl parathion	160
Diuron	270	Maneb	99	Toxaphene	58
Atrazine	190	Captan	115	Carbofuran	454
Trifluralin	150			Carbaryl	153
Paraquat	460			Phorate	172
2,4-D	85				
2,4,5-T	135				
Chloramben	170				
Dinoseb	80				
Propanil	220				
Propachlor	290				
Dicamba	295				
Glyphosate	454				
Diquat	400				

Source: Green 1976.

Table 7 shows the total energy inputs for the pesticides most commonly used in the United States. These figures are for 100 percent active ingredient, but formulation adds only about 2 to 5 GJ/t active ingredient unless large quantities of some particularly complex formulating agent are used. Packaging and transport of pesticides consume only a negligible amount of energy.

These values enable an estimate to be made of the indirect fossil fuel energy which goes, as agrochemicals, into primary crop production. The amount of direct energy which is used in tractors, combine harvesters, and other mechanized equipment is known from many studies carried out by agricultural advisory and extension services in many countries. The amounts of fuel used for all common mechanical operations on the farm have been assessed and the fossil fuel energy used in manufacturing, maintaining, and repairing the mechanical equipment is also known and can be allowed for. Some typical figures are shown in tables 8 and 9. These can, of course, vary quite widely according to whether the soil is light or heavy, whether the weather is wet or dry, and whether the ground is flat or hilly.

Table 8. Energy Input for Tractors (MJ/hr)

37.3 kw (50 h.p.)	190
48.5 kw (65 h.p.)	230
67.2 kw (90 h.p.)	420

Source: Leach 1976.

Table 9. Energy Input for Farming Operations (MJ/ha)

Ploughing (0.2 m depth)	1180
Secondary cultivation	390
Rotary cultivation (deep)	1430
Light cultivation	240
Drilling/harrowing	240
Spraying	73
Combine harvesting	880
Mowing grass	295
Baling hay	295

Source: Leach 1976.

In a similar way, the total fossil fuel energy content of everything else that goes into primary agricultural production can be assessed, whether it is direct energy such as electricity for lighting barns or operating milking machines or indirect energy used to produce string, wire, fencing posts, or any materials used in farming. Irrigation, for example, consumes, on the average, 10 MJ/t if piped water supplies are available but can require much more energy if water is less accessible. In Israel, for example, an average of 200 GJ/ha/yr of fossil fuel are used for irrigation.

Table 10 gives an estimate of the total fossil fuel energy which goes into the total crop production of both the United States and the United Kingdom.

Table 10. Energy Inputs to Crop Production (MGJ)

	U.S. total crops (1970)		U.K. total crops (1972)	
Direct use of fuel	686	44%	83.7	35%
Fertilizers	370	24%	91.2	38%
Pesticides	24	1.6%	2.1	0.9%
Machinery	303	20%	30.2	13%
Irrigation, transport, and miscellaneous	160	10%	29.8	13%
	1543		237	

Source: Blaxter 1975, Steinhart & Steinhart 1974, and U.S. and U.K. government statistics.

Having obtained these figures it is now possible to consider how efficiently energy is used in the various aspects of primary crop production. We shall first consider the indirect energy put in as agrochemicals.

Pesticides account for a very small proportion—of the order of 2 percent—of the total energy put into primary crop

Photo 2A. Young winter wheat plants choked with black grass. (Courtesy of Imperial Chemical Industries Limited.)

production. Although the overall benefits of crop protection have been discussed, it is difficult to state precisely in individual cases that a certain amount of energy put in as pesticides resulted in gain of a specific amount of metabolizable food energy because of the increased crop yields resulting from removal of competition from weeds or prevention of damage by insects and fungi. There is an enormously wide variation in individual cases. At one extreme, use of a pesticide may prevent the total destruction of a crop while, at the other, a pesticidal spray may be applied to guard against the possibility of a pest attack which might or might not occur. If it does not occur, then the pesticide was unnecessary. Between these two extremes, there are a whole range of partial or total crop losses prevented or yield increases produced by judicious use of

Photo 2B. Young winter wheat plants in same field treated with herbicide. (Courtesy of Imperial Chemical Industries Limited.)

pesticides. Nevertheless, in general, the metabolically utilizable energy gained by using pesticides far exceeds the fossil fuel energy contents of those pesticides. For example, corn in the United States requires an energy input of 29.98 GJ/ha if pesticides are used and 29.57 GJ/ha if they are not. If the assumption is made that the yield would be reduced by 10 percent if pesticides were not used—and this is probably a minimum estimate (see figure 7)—then it would be necessary to grow 1.11 ha of nontreated corn to obtain the same amount of product as that from 1 ha of corn treated with pesticides. The energy needed to grow this 1.11 ha would be 32.85 GJ, compared with 29.98 GJ for the 1 ha of treated corn. Pesticide treatment, therefore, in this case, saves 2.87 GJ/ha, which is equivalent to 19 gal of oil per ha. The total number of hectares of corn grown in the

United States is 30 million, so the total annual saving of energy from use of pesticides, assuming an average 10 percent increase in yield from treated crops, is 86 MGJ or about 570 million gal of oil, assuming that the same total output is required.

A typical pesticide spray at 1 kg active ingredient per ha utilizes a total of 263 MJ of energy for its production and application. Table 11 shows the weights of a number of common foodstuffs which would supply 263 MJ of metabolically utilizable food energy—that is, the weights which would compensate in energy terms for the energy put in.

Table 11. Metabolically Utilizable Energy for Various Crops

Crop condition	Metabolically utilizable energy (MJ/kg)	Weight of crop yielding 263 MJ (kg)
Wheat, unprocessed	14.95	17.6
Barley, unprocessed	13.10	18.0
Potatoes, raw	3.18	83.7
Sugar beet, unprocessed	2.64	99.6
Peas, cooked	2.05	128.2
Broad beans, cooked	2.89	91.0
Apples, raw	1.92	137.0
Cabbage, raw	1.17	224.8
Carrots, raw	0.96	274.0
Celery, raw	0.33	797.0
Mushrooms, cooked	0.30	876.7

Source: Price Jones, personal communication.

So, for example, in order to compensate in energy terms for a pesticide applied at 1 kg/ha to wheat, it is necessary to obtain 17.6 kg/ha extra crop. A typical wheat yield in the United Kingdom is 4,300 kg/ha, so 17.6 kg represents a yield increase of only 0.4 percent. Even with a comparatively low-energy-yielding crop such as peas, which typically yield about 3,000 kg/ha, the yield increase needed to compensate in energy terms for use of pesticide is still only 4.3 percent.

The crop losses prevented or the crop yield increases obtained by use of pesticides are generally very much larger than those which would be needed to compensate for the energy input of the pesticide. Manufacture and use of pesticides is, therefore, a very efficient way to utilize fossil fuel energy. By using a comparatively small amount of such energy, which represents past sunshine, we can greatly increase the amount of present sunshine which we can make use of because, by increasing crop yields or preventing crop losses, we increase the total amount of photosynthesis and thus the total amount of present solar energy which is turned into metabolically utilizable food energy for men and animals.

When we consider the energy input:output situation for fertilizer use we have the same problem as with pesticides: there is a great variation in individual cases. Nevertheless, much more accurate assessment is possible because a crop always requires a certain amount of nitrogen, phosphorus, and potassium, whereas attack by pests and diseases is a matter of chance. Also, the increases in yields obtained by using various amounts of fertilizers can be assessed by experiments comparing treated and untreated plots side by side in the same locality and under the same climatic conditions. Many studies have been made of the response of crops to fertilizers so there is a considerable mass of information on this subject. Two examples are given in figures 8 and 9.

Let us consider, as we did with pesticides, corn production in the United States. Corn in the United States requires an energy input of 29.98 GJ/ha if fertilizers are used and 19.05

RESPONSE OF SPRING BARLEY
TO FERTILISER

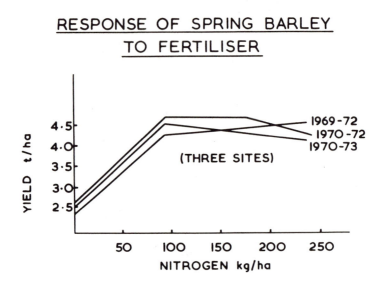

Figure 8. Response of spring barley to fertilizer. *Source:* U.K. Ministry of Agriculture, Fisheries and Food 1974.

GJ/ha if fertilizers are not used. Trials have shown that an average yield of corn treated with fertilizer equivalent in energy terms to 10.93 GJ/ha is about 5,000 kg/ha, whereas an average yield from untreated corn is about 2,000 kg/ha. It would therefore be necessary to grow 2.5 ha of untreated corn to obtain the same amount of product as that from 1 ha of corn treated with fertilizer. The energy needed to grow this 2.5 ha would be 47.6 GJ compared with 29.98 GJ for the 1 ha of treated corn. Fertilizer treatment in this case, therefore, saves 25.2 GJ/ha, which is equivalent to 166 gal of oil per ha. The total number of hectares of corn grown in the United States is 30 million, so the total annual saving of energy from use of fertilizers, assuming that the same total output is required, is 760 MGJ or about 5 billion gal of oil. This energy saving is not, however, the only consideration. For the United States to have produced the

RESPONSE OF GRASS
TO FERTILISER

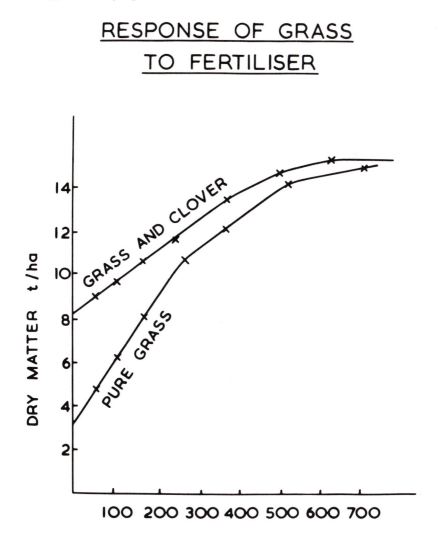

Figure 9. Response of grass to fertilizer. *Source:* Reid 1970.

total amount of corn obtained in 1974 using only the 1945 energy input would have required 2.5 times as much land

and 5 times as much labor; there would have been, in fact, much less corn produced and it would have been very much more expensive. Effectively, the extra energy that was put into corn production between 1945 and 1974 released 20 M ha of land, most of which has been used to grow soy beans. From the farmer's point of view, fertilizer use is an excellent financial proposition since every $1 spent on fertilizer for corn in 1974 gave $11 worth of extra yield.

Table 12. Average Fertilizer Usage for Various Crops

Crop	Average fertilizer used (kg/ha)			Average energy put in as fertilizer (GJ/ha)
	N	P	K	
Corn (U.S.)	125	51	51	10.93
Rice (U.S.)	134	67	. .	11.66
Wheat (U.K.)	130	50	50	11.67
Barley (U.K.)	97	48	48	8.86
Potatoes (U.K.)	175	175	250	18.80
Sugar beet (U.K.)	160	50	150	14.85
Carrots (U.K.)	82	105	105	8.97
Peas (U.K.)	. .	50	50	1.15
Broad beans (U.K.)	17	138	138	4.51

Source: U.S. and U.K. government statistics.

The effects of fertilizer on corn have been studied in very great detail. From the dosage response curve for nitrogen fertilizers it has been deduced that, when all the fossil fuel energy used in production, packaging, transport, and application of the fertilizer is taken into account, the energy output:input ratio is 8.86 for the first 50 kg/ha of nitrogen applied, falling to 5.95 for the fourth 50 kg/ha. This illustrates that application of fertilizers is subject to the law of diminishing returns and that one cannot go on increasing crop yields per ha indefinitely by applying more and more fertilizer. In developed countries we have probably reached the peak of utility for application of fertilizer and, in some cases, we may well have gone beyond it.

As with pesticides, we can draw up a table showing the weights of common foodstuffs which would supply metabolically utilizable food energy equivalent in amount to the fossil fuel energy normally put into each crop as fertilizer. To do this, it is necessary to know how much fertilizer is normally applied to each crop at the present time. This information is given in table 12. The weights of crop equivalent to these amounts of fertilizer are shown in table 13 along with the average increase in yield per ha which use of fertilizer is known, from controlled trials, to produce in each crop.

Table 13. Metabolically Utilizable Energy for Various Crops

Crop	Metabolically utilizable energy (MJ/kg)	Weight of crop yielding energy equivalent to fertilizer used (kg)	Increase in yield produced by fertilizer (kg/ha)
Corn (U.S.)	15.19	720	3000
Rice (U.S.)	14.80	788	4000
Wheat (U.K.)	14.95	781	1500
Barley (U.K.)	13.10	676	1500
Potatoes (U.K.)	3.18	5912	13000
Sugar beet (U.K.)	2.64	5625	14000
Carrots (U.K.)	0.96	934	3000
Peas (U.K.)	2.05	561	1000
Broad beans (U.K.)	2.89	1560	2000

Source: U.S. and U.K. government statistics.

The energy output:input ratio for fertilizer use therefore generally lies between two and four. As with pesticides, the use of the energy of past sunshine stored in fossil fuels enables us greatly to increase the amount of present solar energy converted by plants into metabolically utilizable food energy for men and animals.

Table 14. Crop Production in the United Kingdom (1952 = 100)

	1952	1960	1965	1968	1970	1972	1975
Total fossil fuel energy input	100	119	135	157	164	170	177
Yield of wheat per ha (5-yr average)	100	123	138	150	160	167	175
Total value of all crops grown	100	120	137	143	152	164	173
Total number of man-years	100	81	67	59	56	54	50
Value of crops produced per man-year	100	148	204	242	271	304	346
Value of crops produced per unit of fossil fuel energy put in	100	101	101	91	93	96	98

Source: Leach 1976 and U.K. government statistics.

Direct use of fossil fuels in primary crop production mainly has an effect on crop yields per man-hour rather than on crop yields per ha. Given the same amounts of fertilizers and pesticides it would be theoretically possible to produce the same amount of crops from the same amount of land if you could put enough people to work on that land. To produce 1975 output of crops in the United States with the 1945 degree of mechanization would require the agricultural labor force to be increased fivefold. Manual labor costs $6,000 per GJ whereas fossil fuel costs only $15 per GJ. The effect of any substantial decrease in the amount of mechanization of U.S. farms would be a very steep rise in the cost of food, almost certainly to levels which would be quite unacceptable to the U.S. consumer who might well find that, in such circumstances, he would need to spend 50%-60% of his take-home pay on food, instead of the 20% he now spends.

The total effect over the past thirty years of putting increasing amounts of fossil fuel energy into primary crop production, both directly as fuel for mechanical equipment and indirectly as agrochemicals, has been to increase yields per ha, to increase the total amount and value of crops grown, and to decrease the amount of labor needed. These trends are illustrated by the figures in table 14.

The most significant effect from the point of view of the community is that the value of crops produced has increased by 73 percent in 25 years and that the value of crops produced per man-year has increased 3.5 times during that period. The value of crops produced per unit of fossil fuel put in remained virtually steady. The price of fossil fuel rose considerably during the period indicating that the use of fossil fuel to grow crops was getting steadily less economical. However, it has a very long way to go before it is no longer profitable.

The conclusion may be reached that, in primary production of crops, the output of metabolically utilizable food energy generally considerably exceeds the input of fossil fuel energy, so that growing crops is an efficient way in which to make use of this energy. Typical input:output figures for various crops are shown in table 15.

However, when we include raising of animals and calculate the energy outputs and inputs for agriculture as a whole, the energy utilization picture looks much less favorable. The figures for the United States over the years 1940 to 1970 are shown in table 16 and those for the United Kingdom over the years 1952 to 1972 in table 17.

Table 15. Energy Output:Input for Various Crops

Crop	Net edible yield (t/ha/yr)	Energy content (MJ/kg)	Energy output (GJ/ha/yr)	Energy input (GJ/ha/yr)	Output:input ratio
Barley, U.K. 1968-72	3.4	10.9	37.2	15.7	2.4
Wheat, U.K. 1968-72	3.9	14.4	56.2	17.8	3.4
Potatoes, U.K. 1968-72	17.9	3.2	56.9	36.2	1.6
Sugar beet, U.K. 1968-72	35.5	2.8	99.1	27.4	3.6
Grass (grazing only)	13.3	10.6	141.0	38.2	3.7
Grass (grazing and one cut hay)	8.3	10.6	60.0	12.7	4.7
Corn, U.S. 1970-74	5.1	15.2	76.9	29.9	2.6
Rice, U.S. 1970-74	5.7	14.8	84.1	65.5	1.3

Source: Leach 1976.

The reason for the poor energy output:input ratios for agriculture as a whole compared with those for production of crops is that raising of animals is a very energy-inefficient process. Animals are very poor converters of the food energy they consume into edible human foodstuffs such as meat, milk, and eggs. Fossil fuel energy has to be used to grow vast amounts of feedstuffs for animals, more fossil fuel energy has to be used to rear and maintain the animals, and only a comparatively small proportion of this total energy put in is returned as metabolically utilizable food energy for humans.

Table 16. Energy Inputs to Total U.S. Agriculture (MGJ)

	1940	1950	1960	1970
Direct use of fuel	296	800	981	1239
Agrochemicals	52	101	172	394
Machinery	45	137	225	343
Irrigation, transport, and miscellaneous	129	238	189	228
Total energy input	522	1276	1567	2204
Total energy output	1180	1417	1641	1911
Energy output:input ratio	2.26	1.12	1.05	0.87

Source: Steinhart and Steinhart 1974.

Table 17. Energy Inputs to Total U.K. Agriculture (MGJ)

	1950	1960	1965	1968	1970	1972
Direct use of fuel	87.8	89.3	102.5	108.4	113.8	126.8
Agrochemicals	28.0	51.3	64.7	81.9	87.1	93.3
Machinery, irrigation, transport, and miscellaneous	49.7	59.9	72.1	83.2	88.6	95.9
Import and transport of animal feedstuffs	75.5	86.5	85.7	104.5	106.5	94.0
Total energy input	241	287	325	378	396	410
Total energy output	99	112	117	130	135	138
Energy output:input ratio	0.41	0.39	0.36	0.34	0.34	0.34

Source: Leach 1976.

For example (Blaxter 1975), in the United Kingdom in 1972, 237 MGJ fossil fuel energy were put into primary production of crops and produced plant material with a total metabolic energy content of 1,116 MGJ, an energy out-put:input ratio of 4.7. Of this plant material, the equivalent of 997 MGJ were used as animal feedstuffs. Nine hundred fifty-one MGJ actually went into animals and 46 MGJ were wasted. Only 119 MGJ of plant material went directly for human consumption and gave 65 MGJ of edible plant food. The fossil fuel energy used to grow this food was 25.3 MGJ, so the energy output:input ratio for human vegetable food was 2.6. The 951 MGJ fed to animals was supplemented by 104 MGJ of imported feedstuffs and produced 73 MGJ of edible animal food. The fossil fuel energy used to rear and maintain the animals was 103 MGJ and the fossil fuel energy used to grow or import the animal feed was 282 MGJ, a total of 385 MGJ to obtain 73 MGJ of edible animal food, thus an energy output:input ratio of only 0.19.

The energy output:input ratios for various animal products are shown in table 18.

Table 18. Energy Output:Input Ratio for Animal Products

Product	Output:input ratio
Feed-fed beef (U.S.)	0.1
Grass-fed beef (U.S.)	0.3
Intensive eggs (U.S.)	0.2
Milk (U.S.)	0.5
Pigs (U.K.)	0.3
Poultry meat (U.K.)	0.1
Intensive eggs (U.K.)	0.14
Milk (U.K.)	0.37

Source: Leach 1976, and Steinhart and Steinhart 1974.

These figures indicate that the overall situation is not much different in the United States from that in the United Kingdom nor, for that matter, in most developed countries. The reason for the greater energy efficiency of milk production in the United States compared with the United Kingdom is that more land is available per head of cattle in the United States. To produce 10,000 l of milk on 3 ha requires an energy input of 35 GJ, but to produce the same amount on 2 ha requires 47 GJ.

The figures in table 18 should be compared with those for crop production in table 15. The comparison shows just how profligate in the use of fossil fuel energy is the production of animal products. Fishing is no answer as the energy output:input ratios are even worse than for animal production, ranging from 0.08 for U.S. offshore fishing through 0.05 for U.K. deep-sea fishing, and 0.01 for small-boat fishing in the Adriatic to 0.006 for shrimps in the Gulf of Mexico.

It can be seen why meat and fish are expensive but in an affluent society the consumer likes meat and fish and is able and willing to pay to obtain them. It is not the purpose of this book to argue the case for a vegetarian diet. There are many more things to be taken into account in this argument besides energy. Animals can feed off land unsuitable for cultivation of crops such as the rough hill grazing land which accounts for a third of the total agricultural area of the United Kingdom, or the rangelands of the American West. When raised in these areas, animals are not very energy-demanding. So the energy output:input ratio for range-fed beef in the United States is about two and for sheep in Scotland in the United Kingdom about three. These energy output:input ratios are favorable for precisely the same reason that the energy output:input ratio for the Kung bushmen was about eight: because the amount of land used was large. One can always reduce the amount of fossil fuel energy needed to achieve a given output of crops or animals and improve the energy output:input ratio by using more land—provided that the land is available. Raising cattle on rangeland or sheep on hillsides is a good way to use these types of land but the output per ha is small and quite insufficient to meet the needs of populations of the size of those in the developed countries. Thus, to feed the whole population of the United States on range-fed beef would require 25 ha of range per head of population which is about ten times the total amount of agricultural land actually available in the United States. It is the intensive production of animal products needed to meet the demands of the population for a mixed animal and vegetable diet which requires large energy inputs.

The fact is that at present the consumer in an affluent country such as the United States will continue to demand and get what he wants, as long as he can pay for it. The question can reasonably be asked, "Is it wrong that fossil fuel energy should be used to give the nation a varied diet?" To answer this question, and to see the matter in its true light, we must consider what proportion of the total fossil fuel energy used by the nation is actually used to grow crops and to rear animals—that is, for primary agricultural production up to the farm gate.

In 1970, the total amount of fossil fuel energy used in the United States for primary agricultural production was 3.1 percent of the total fossil fuel used in that year in the United States for all purposes. In 1972 in the United Kingdom the figure was 4.6 percent. These figures put into a proper perspective all the arguments and discussions about the amounts of fossil fuel energy used in primary agricultural production. Even if all that energy could be saved, it would make very little difference to the present drain on the world's fossil fuel resources. Every man, woman, and child in the United States preempts every day the equivalent of 6.4 gal of oil of which only 0.23 gal are used for primary production of his or her food and 6.17 gal for other purposes. In the United Kingdom every man, woman, and child preempts the equivalent of 2.8 gal of oil every day of which only 0.12 gal are used for primary production of his or her food and 2.68 gal for other purposes.

As long as any nation indulges in unrestrained private motoring, overheating, overcooling, or overilluminating its buildings, unrestricted manufacture of a great deal of unnecessary junk, and preparation for war, then that nation's priorities are dreadfully wrong if it tries to cut down the comparatively small amount of energy which is used to produce its essential food while continuing to squander energy recklessly elsewhere.

The energy output:input ratio for primary agricultural production is 0.87 in the United States and 0.34 in the United Kingdom. This means that primary agricultural production in the United States operates at a thermal efficiency of 87 percent, and in the United Kingdom at 34 percent. By comparison, the thermal efficiency of electricity production is about 30 percent and of the average internal combustion engine is about 25%-35% according to compression ratio. The total proportion of the nation's energy which is used for primary agricultural production is small and better utilized than most of the energy expended in other ways. Certainly we should try to economize on energy used in primary agricultural production and to use it more efficiently, but it is clear that we must look elsewhere for large savings of energy. One of the places we need to look is the rest of the nation's food system, since food at the farm gate has a long way to go before it reaches the dining table.

CHAPTER THREE

Energy in Food Processing, Distribution, and Preparation

Very few crops nowadays are taken from the farm and sold directly to the consumer without cleaning, packaging, or other preparation. Even the crops that go straight from farmer to consumer have to be picked up from the farmer, taken to the wholesale markets, and distributed from there to the retailers. Most crops are subjected to some form of processing. Thus, root crops such as potatoes, carrots, and turnips may be cleaned, graded, and prepacked into plastic bags and then often frozen; or they may be canned. Some may be further converted into convenience products such as instant mashed potatoes or potato chips. Vegetables such as cabbage and cauliflower are generally cleaned and prepacked; peas are shelled, graded, and frozen or canned; green beans are cleaned, sliced, and frozen. Fruit is cleaned, graded, prepacked, often canned, and sometimes frozen, and some is further processed to make jams, purees, and piefillings. Cereals have to be milled and baked into bread, cake, cookies, and similar confectionery. All these crop products are further converted and combined into a vast range of convenience foods—instant breakfasts, cake and cookie mixes, ready-prepared dinners, and similar products— which are being made increasingly more fancy and packaged more ornately to catch the eye of the consumer in a very competitive industry. Novelty and convenience foods are becoming more and more artificial and sophisticated in order to give them "added value." This may make economic sense but it uses up energy and does not add at all to the nutritional value of the product.

Fresh meat needs refrigeration and preparation for retail sale. Bacon has to be cured and sausages have to be fabricated. Meat is converted to a wide variety of pies, patties, hamburgers, and also extensively processed to give a range of canned meats. Milk is pasteurized and packed in bottles or cartons and is also converted into dairy products such as butter, cheese, and yogurt. Eggs are collected, graded, and packed.

The brewing industry takes cereals and sugar (which has to be extracted from sugarcane or sugar beet) and subjects them to complex processes to provide a variety of alcoholic beverages. The soft drink industry likewise uses crop products on a massive scale to manufacture popular beverages.

In all cases the crop or animal products have to be picked up from the various farms, or from the ports if they come from overseas, transported to the processing factories, distributed from there to the wholesalers and then to the retailers, and picked up from the retailers by the consumers who may be in households, restaurants, industrial cafeterias, or the kitchens of public institutions. Having reached the consumer, they have still to be stored, prepared, cooked, and served. At all locations from farm through food factory, from wholesaler and retailer to consumer there is garbage

Table 19. Energy Input to Postfarm U.K. Food System, 1970

	Energy input (MGJ)	Energy per person (GJ)	Percentage of nation's total energy use
Food processing	430	7.7	5.0
Drink processing	115	2.0	1.3
Distribution to and by retailers	144	2.6	1.7
Use of cars in food-related business	84	1.5	0.9
Consumer shopping	195	3.5	2.3
Food preparation and cooking (restaurants and cafeterias)	230	4.1	2.7
Food preparation and cooking (home)	500	9.0	5.8
Garbage and sewage disposal	62	1.1	0.7
Construction and maintenance of food-related buildings	205	3.9	2.4
TOTAL	1965	35.2	22.8
Primary agricultural production	*396*	*7.1*	*4.6*

Source: Leach 1976 and U.K. government statistics.

and refuse to be collected and disposed of, and sewage from the final consumer. At every stage in all these operations of processing, distribution, and preparation, which together make up the nation's food system, fossil fuel energy is fed in.

The figures for the postfarm U.K. food system for 1970 are shown in table 19 and the figures for the postfarm U.S.

Table 20. Energy Input to Postfarm U.S. Food System, 1970

	Energy input (MGJ)	Energy per person (GJ)	Percentage of nation's total energy use
Food processing	1942	9.5	2.7
Drink processing	473	2.3	0.7
Distribution to and by retailers	1113	5.5	1.6
Use of cars on food-related business	523	2.6	0.7
Consumer shopping	1353	6.6	1.9
Food preparation and cooking (restaurants and cafeterias)	1190	5.8	1.7
Food preparation and cooking (home)	2179	10.7	3.1
Garbage and sewage disposal	231	1.1	0.3
Construction and maintenance of food-related buildings	838	4.1	1.2
TOTAL	9842	48.2	13.8
Primary agricultural production	*2204*	*10.8*	*3.1*

Source: Steinhart and Steinhart 1974, and U.S. government statistics.

food system in 1970 in table 20. To facilitate comparison, the figures for energy inputs to primary agricultural production are put in italics at the bottom of each table.

The first thing to note is that the proportion of the nation's energy which is used to process, distribute, and prepare food is much greater than that which is used to grow or produce it. For the United Kingdom, the figures are 22.5 percent of the nation's total energy used postfarm compared with only 4.6 percent on the farm, a ratio of five to one. For the United States, the figures are 13.8 percent of the nation's total energy used postfarm compared with 3.1 percent on the farm, a ratio of just over four to one.

The fact that the United States used 16.9 percent of the nation's total energy in the total food system in 1970 whereas the United Kingdom used 27.4 percent is not an indication of greater efficiency and economy in the United States but simply that the United States uses vastly greater total amounts of fossil fuel energy than the United Kingdom. The economic situation of the United Kingdom requires that country to direct a considerable proportion of the total fossil fuel energy which it uses to the purpose of feeding its population. The United States, a much more affluent country, can afford to lavish fossil fuel energy on many other things. This becomes clear when we look at the amounts of energy used per person in each country. Each person in the United Kingdom in 1970 used 7.1 GJ of fossil fuel energy to grow or produce food and 35.2 GJ to process, distribute, and prepare it. Each person in the United States in 1970 used 10.8 GJ of fossil fuel energy to grow or produce food and 48.2 GJ to process, distribute, and prepare it. The United States uses about 40 percent more fossil fuel energy per person in its food system than does the United Kingdom, a reflection of the relative prosperities of the two countries.

Food Processing

When we were considering primary agricultural production, we introduced the concept of energy output:input ratio as a measure of the efficiency with which fossil fuel energy was being utilized. This was an appropriate and useful concept because a certain amount of fossil fuel energy is put into the primary agricultural system, producing a certain amount of metabolically utilizable food energy in the form of crops or animals. However, anything that is done to the crop or animal product after it leaves the farm gate cannot increase its metabolically utilizable food energy and, in practice, will probably decrease it as a result of inevitable wastage. The energy output:input concept is, therefore, not meaningful for the postfarm processing, distribution, and preparation system considered on its own since from an energy-balance viewpoint all the energy put into the food system after the farm gate is completely unproductive. Still, it does serve the useful and necessary purpose of getting the food to the people and presenting it to them in digestible, palatable, and acceptable forms.

The reasons why so much fossil fuel energy is used in food processing, distribution, and preparation are almost entirely economic. The traders and businessmen who are involved in the various operations in the postfarm food system use fossil fuel energy for exactly the same reason that the farmer does: because it has proved highly profitable to them to do so. The difference is that the farmers obtain their profits by using fossil fuel energy to produce more product from a given area of land. They do not actually increase the value per t of what they grow; they grow more of it. In contrast to this, the middlemen obtain their profits by using fossil fuel energy to give "added value" to the food products—that is, to take a comparatively cheap food product and titivate it up in some way so that it can be sold at a higher price. They do not increase the amount of a product; they increase its value.

The energy output:input concept can, however, be applied

to any food product at any stage in its processing, distribution, and preparation, right up to its consumption. This is done by comparing the metabolically utilizable food energy content of the product with the total amount of fossil fuel energy used to produce the product, to put it into whatever form it has reached at that stage, and to bring it to its location at that stage. By this means the relative efficiencies in energy terms of getting, say, some fresh eggs, a loaf of bread, and a can of peas alongside one another in the same supermarket can be assessed.

Some figures of this type for some common foodstuffs in the United Kingdom are shown in table 21. (The picture probably would not be very different in the United States.) Energy output:input ratios are shown for the products at the stage when they have been processed into their final form and are either ready to eat or ready to cook, but have not yet been distributed to wholesalers and retailers for sale to the ultimate consumers. For comparison, the total energy input for production of an average U.S. automobile is shown in italics.

Note in table 21 that the high energy output:input ratios achieved by modern intensive cereal growing (wheat, 3.4; corn, 2.6) have been reduced by the milling and baking operations needed to convert them to an edible, salable product to around 0.5 (bread, 0.47; cornflakes, 0.70). This brings them more in line with the animal products milk and butter (milk, 0.33; butter, 0.34). However, the energy output:input ratios for processed cereal products are still considerably greater than those for intensively raised meat (beef, 0.09; chicken, 0.09), although the energy output:input ratio for range-fed beef would almost certainly be comparable or better. Still, cereal products and milk are ready to eat, whereas meat needs cooking either commercially or

Table 21. Energy Inputs to Processed Foods
in the United Kingdom, 1970

	Total energy input for production, processing, and packaging (GJ/t)	Metabolizable food energy output (GJ/t)	Energy output:input ratio
Bread	22.8	10.8	0.47
Biscuits (cookies)	46.8	19.2	0.41
Cornflakes	22.4	15.7	0.70
Sugar	25.8	16.0	0.65
Chocolate	54.9	21.9	0.40
Margarine	23.6	32.2	1.36
Peas (fresh)	2.8	2.5	0.89
Peas (deep frozen)	3.2	2.5	0.78
Peas (canned)	30.4	2.5	0.08
Fruit (fresh)	1.5	1.2	0.80
Fruit (deep frozen)	1.7	1.2	0.70
Fruit (canned in syrup)	27.6	3.2	0.12
Milk	7.6	2.5	0.33
Butter	90.3	31.2	0.34
Eggs	50.2	6.6	0.13
Fresh beef	115.5	10.3	0.09
Frozen chicken (intensive-reared)	60.5	5.6	0.09
Meat (canned)	134.8	10.0	0.07
Fish (canned)	27.3	6.8	
Soft drinks	20.6	3.0	0.15
Beer	19.2	2.4	0.13
Spirits	46.4	10.3	0.22
Average U.S. automobile 300		. .	. .

Source: Trade Association Statistics.

at home, which consumes a lot of energy.

Note, too, in table 21 that fresh vegetables and fruit have an energy output:input ratio less than 1. Although the energy requirements to grow fruit and vegetables are not large, their metabolically utilizable food energy contents are generally small. A point to be considered in any discussion of animal versus vegetable food is that animal and processed cereal foods are high-energy foods whereas fruit and vegetables are low-energy foods. Deep-freezing of fruit and vegetables does not add very much to the energy requirements, but the process of canning is extremely energy-demanding. Thus the energy output:input ratio for canned peas falls to 0.08 and for canned fruit to 0.12. It is, of course, relatively much more wasteful of energy to can low-energy foods such as vegetables than to can high-energy foods such as meat. This is illustrated by the figures in table 22.

Table 22. Energy to Produce 568 cm^3 (20 oz) Can

	Energy input (MJ)	Energy output (MJ)	Energy output:input ratio
Apples in syrup	6.9	0.6	0.09
Peaches in syrup	7.4	1.1	0.15
Carrots in brine	6.9	0.3	0.03
Peas	7.9	1.4	0.18
Tomatoes	6.6	0.2	0.03
Asparagus spears	6.9	0.3	0.04
Baked beans	8.9	2.1	0.24
Pilchards	11.6	5.1	0.44
Beef stew	9.8	3.3	0.34

Source: Hawthorn 1975.

A final point to note from table 21 is that beverages do not fare very well on an energy output:input basis, regardless of whether they are hard or soft drinks (beer, 0.13; cola, 0.15).

Some further examples of the relative amounts of fossil fuel energy used in different types of processing are given in table 23 for a number of meat products.

Table 23. Energy to Produce Meat Products (GJ/t)

Fresh pork (boned and skinned)	27.3
Vacuum packed bacon	43.2
Pork sausages	41.3
Pork pies	27.5
Boned beef, joints, vacuum packed	32.3
Factory roast joints, vacuum packed	57.5
Meat pies, excluding pork pies	42.3

Source: Trade Association Statistics.

The figures in tables 21, 22, and 23 are approximate average figures covering a wide variety of commercial products. Energy requirements in food processing vary enormously; some processes are very economical in energy use while others are profligate. Little purpose would be served by trying to go into greater detail than is shown by the figures in table 21 because the conclusions might be misleading and would almost certainly show a very wide spread of energy requirements within any one broad category of food processing. It is the overall national picture which is the significant matter for consideration.

However, a different approach can take the analysis further. All food processing contains three elements: transport, the processing itself, and packaging. In table 24 the

Table 24. Energy Inputs for Processing of Foods
in the United Kingdom, 1970

	Transport (MGJ)	Actual processing (MGJ)	Packaging (MGJ)
Milling grain	2.3	15.2	3.1
Animal food	3.0	30.8	8.5
Bread and flour	7.1	43.5	8.3
Biscuits	1.4	26.2	1.1
Cornflakes and starch products	1.4	23.2	11.0
Sugar	1.7	30.7	1.3
Chocolate	1.8	31.2	12.9
Margarine	0.2	4.7	1.2
Fruit and vegetables*	2.3	30.8	24.9
Milk and products	4.7	34.8	13.2
Butter and cheese	0.7	12.0	0.7
Eggs	0.8	..	2.4
Meat, fish, and products*	3.4	21.7	9.3
Soft drinks	2.1	13.4	8.3
Beer	4.6	44.8	8.1
Wine and spirits	0.9	17.8	11.4
	38.4	380.8	125.7
	7%	70%	23%

Source: Chapman 1975 and Leach 1976.
*Includes canned products.

breakdown is shown for the main categories of food processing in the United Kingdom in 1970.

Most important in this table is the relatively large amounts of energy used in packaging. The very high energy requirement for canning is reflected in the figures for fruit and vegetables, which indicate that 43 percent of the total energy used in the processing of these foodstuffs goes into packaging. Even if it is reasonable to use considerable amounts of irreplaceable and limited fossil fuel reserves to can fruit and vegetables, there is absolutely no justification for using them to can pet foods, which are produced and marketed on a vast and increasing scale. The only reason for this is that the pet food industry finds it profitable.

Likewise, packaging of liquids such as milk, soft drinks, beer, and spirits into glass bottles or plastic containers is energy-demanding. This is true also for the low-calorie soft drinks. Only an extremely affluent nation can use large amounts of irreplaceable and limited fossil fuel energy to package "slimming" foods and drinks containing practically no nourishment while millions of people in the developing countries are undernourished or starving.

Table 25 shows the total national energy usages for processing foodstuffs in the United States and United Kingdom in 1970.

Table 25. Energy Inputs for Processing of Foods, 1970

	Transport (MGJ)	Actual processing (MGJ)	Packaging (MGJ)	Total (MGJ)
U.K.	38 (7%)	381 (70%)	126 (23%)	545
U.S.	232 (10%)	1315 (54%)	868 (36%)	2415

Source: Leach 1976, and Steinhart and Steinhart 1974.

The U.K. usage is 9.7 GJ per person and 6.3 percent of total U.K. energy use and the U.S. usage is 11.8 GJ per person and 3.4 percent of total U.S. energy use. In the United Kingdom, 23 percent of the total energy used in food processing went on packaging. In the United States, the figure for packaging was 36 percent: steel and aluminum cans 21 percent, glass containers 8 percent, and paper and plastic packings 7 percent. Although some packaging is obviously necessary to contain and distribute foodstuffs it is pertinent to ask whether, for commercial and advertising reasons, this has now gone beyond reasonable bounds. Some food products are as much as triple-wrapped.

A source of actual loss of fossil fuel energy in processing—a use of energy without getting anything in return—is physical wastage or spoilage of the foodstuffs, either during storage and pick-up before processing, or during the processing operation itself. Such losses have the effect of reducing the energy input:output ratio for the nation's food system as a whole.

Table 26. Percentage of Postharvest
Storage Losses on U.K. Farms

Wheat	1
Barley	1
Potatoes	10
Peas	4
Green beans	2
Cabbage	9
Carrots	24
Onions	11
Apples	5

Source: Roy 1976.

Losses on the farm after harvesting but before dispatch have already been taken into account in the figures indicating that U.K. agriculture produced 119 MGJ of plant material intended for human consumption as distinct from feed for animals, but that this gave only 65 MGJ of edible plant food. These losses are accounted for partly by the quantities of crop residue such as leaves and stalks which have to be destroyed or ploughed in, and partly by crops not harvested or ploughed in because of low prices or lack of demand. This particularly affects the growers of fruit and vegetables. For example, in the United Kingdom, 5%-15% of cauliflower grown is left in the field. A further loss is in poorly designed or badly adjusted machinery and unskilled or careless operators which together can result in incomplete harvesting or significant crop damage. This is a special problem for growers of root crops such as sugar beet and potatoes. A survey by the British Sugar Corporation showed an average 8 percent loss of sugar beet with individual losses of up to 50 percent. A survey by the U.K. Potato Marketing Board showed that 21 percent of potatoes grown were so damaged during harvesting that they were unfit for sale. Losses can also occur if a crop is harvested only once, because a proportion of it may at the time be overripe or underripe. This is a problem for fruit growers particularly, but an estimate has also been given that up to 25 percent of peas grown may not be harvested in individual cases.

Losses may also result from attack by pests or diseases during storage before dispatch. Some figures for average losses of various crops in the United Kingdom during post-harvest storage on the farm are shown in table 26; however, much more extensive losses in storage are likely to occur in the silos and warehouses of the food processors.

In large stores, rats and mice are a principal cause of loss, as are insect pests and fungal diseases. Modern storage technology has done much in developed countries to reduce such losses but they can still be extensive for certain commodities.

By and large, cereals are handled very efficiently and losses during transport from farm to processor and in storage do not exceed 0.3%-0.4%. Vegetables and fruits, however, are particularly prone to storage losses and it has been estimated that 5%-8% of main-crop potatoes, 30% of stored carrots, and 25%-45% of winter cabbage are discarded. (Intervention buying and very long-term storage of food products, for example, by the U.S. government or the European Economic Community Agricultural Authority could greatly increase the possibilities of storage losses.)

In food processing itself, losses and wastage vary enormously. Some commodities are handled very efficiently: only 0.3 percent of milk is lost during bottling and only 0.9 percent of eggs are broken in packaging. The animal-products business is well organized in this respect and there is little waste. Swifts in Chicago used to boast that they "used every part of the pig except the squeak," and this is still substantially true. Nevertheless, it is estimated that about 8 percent of all meat is still condemned as unfit for human consumption at the abattoirs, and most of this goes into canned pet foods.

Other food-processing operations are even more wasteful. For example, in fruit and vegetable canning, apart from the very high fossil fuel energy requirements already noted, there are considerable actual losses of edible material. Some figures for the United States are shown in table 27.

Some food processing operations are particularly wasteful because they are entirely aesthetic or cosmetic. An example is the U.S. practice of shaping each root to make carrots of identical shape and size for canning.

The reason for discussing losses, wastage, and spoilage of food during harvesting, storage, transport, and processing is that all food lost at these stages has, by the time that it

Table 27. Percentage of Wastage
in Vegetable and Fruit Canning

Green beans	5	Sweet corn	20
Butter beans	6	Tomatoes	5
Beets	7	Apples	12
Sprouts	10	Pears	12
Cabbage	5	Apricots	8
Carrots	18	Peaches	20
Peas	6	Grapefruit	3
Potatoes	5		

Source: U.S.D.A. 1965.

is lost, accumulated an input of fossil fuel energy. The total effect of such losses is to reduce the energy output: input ratio for the nation's food system as a whole.

Food Distribution

In developed countries where millions of people live together in large cities, it is obvious that there must be an effective system of food distribution if all these people are to be fed. The logistics of transporting vast quantities of food every day into large cities and distributing it to retailers are formidable, and the effectiveness with which it is done is shown by the constantly well-stocked shelves of the supermarkets. However, the criteria determining how this distribution system was built up and how it is operated are entirely economic. The motivation is maximization of individual profit by individual distributors. As energy has been, and still is, comparatively cheap it is used freely. No attempt has been made to evolve a food distribution system that is most economical for the nation as a whole and, in particular, no attempt has been made to use energy as economically and efficiently as possible on a national scale in food distribution. In affluent societies such as the United States in which a majority of people can afford to eat what they like, little consideration is given to cost-effectiveness or energy-effectiveness in providing food. The consumer is king, and if he wants greenhouse tomatoes—which have an energy output:input ratio thirty times less than that for wheat—then he gets them. In developed countries food is produced, processed, and distributed in accordance with consumer demand not consumer need.

It may be argued that this is exactly what should happen in a free economy and that, if the price of energy rises as a result of its becoming scarcer, those systems of food distribution which are very energy-demanding will be priced out of the market. The reasons why this may not happen are twofold. Firstly, many food distribution systems are the result of large investments and the people who have made these investments will do everything they can to perpetuate them. Secondly, the consumer in affluent societies will be willing to pay increased prices to gratify his existing tastes in food, even if he has to demand higher wages to be able to do so. Thus there may be a tendency to bolster up food distribution systems which are energy-inefficient but profitable to middlemen and which satisfy consumer demand.

An example (Bleasdale 1976) may be given to illustrate these two points. The Atchison, Topeka and Santa Fe Railroad has a fleet of 5,900 refrigerated units. For an investment of this size in food distribution to be profitable it must be used throughout the year. Consequently, lettuce is transported to the northeastern states from the Pacific coast even though lettuce could be supplied more economically by local growers during the summer. These local growers have been edged out of the market because it is the policy of distributing companies to help clients develop distant markets that will result in more transport and, therefore, increased profits for the distributors. To do this, supplies of lettuce from a distance were sold at a loss over limited periods to force local growers out of business so that the whole market would be secured for the distant producer, who is able to supply throughout the year and thus create continuous business for the distributor. From the point of view of the wholesaler, this insures a higher-quality product because a distant producer cannot afford to pay high transport costs for lettuce of inferior quality even though such lettuce would be acceptable to many customers if offered at a lower price, as it could be if it were grown locally. However, the affluent consumer will pay for appearance even when it is only cosmetic and does not affect the nutritive value of the food.

The second point concerning consumer sovereignty may also be illustrated by the example of lettuce (Bleasdale 1976). If lettuce plants are grown very close together and harvested while still immature they give individual leaves that are succulent, crisp, and tender but are not in the customary form of bunched heads with tight hearts. These immature lettuce require less labor to produce than conventional lettuce and yield twice as much product in half the time. Several crops can be taken during a year and the total metabolically utilizable food energy produced is 76 GJ/ha compared with 77 GJ/ha for corn. The energy output:input ratio is 0.5 for a ready-to-eat product. Nevertheless, replacement of conventional lettuce by this new form is likely to be opposed both by the distributing companies and by conservative consumers, even though such replacements would be energy-saving.

Many other examples of high, and possibly unjustified, use of fossil fuel energy in food distribution could be quoted. The Pacific Fruit Express Company has 10,300 trucks each with its own diesel-electric refrigeration plant and capable of carrying around 60 t of produce. Investment on this scale has to be justified by continuous use. The author has recently seen avocados from California on sale in a Florida supermarket at 39c when similar avocados could be bought from local growers in neighborhood shops at 24c. Some consumers will, however, willingly pay high prices to avoid having to shop around.

Table 28. Energy Input for Distribution of Foods in the United Kingdom, 1970

	MGJ
Fuel and power	83
Capital purchases	7
Packaging	17
Transport	23
Miscellaneous	14
Total	144

Source: Leach 1976.

Thus high investment in distribution systems and established consumer habits make it very difficult to change existing distributive systems. For example, U.K. homemakers would vigorously oppose any attempt to stop daily delivery of milk in glass bottles, which are supposed to be returnable but of which 20 percent are lost, even though U.S. homemakers get their milk from the supermarket in cartons. In order to sustain the profitability of the U.K. system, milk-men now have to sell a range of other, nondairy, products such as bread, potatoes, frozen chicken, and soft drinks.

The total amount of fossil fuel energy used for food distribution by the United Kingdom in 1970 was 144 MGJ (1.7 percent of total U.K. energy use, 2.6 GJ per person) and by the United States in 1970 was 1,113 MGJ (1.6 percent of total U.S. energy, 5.5 GJ per person).

A breakdown of the way in which distribution energy is used in the United Kingdom is shown in table 28. As in processing, packaging is a substantial item accounting for 12 percent of the total energy used in distribution.

By and large, actual losses and wastages during distribution are not great. At the wholesaling stage very little is lost,

Table 29. Percentage of Wastage in
Supermarkets in the United Kingdom

Meat	
bacon	2.1
sausages	1.8
pork	1.7
cooked meats	1.2
meat pies	0.8
other meat	0.1
Eggs	1.3
Fruit and vegetables	0.5
Frozen food	0.2
Canned and packaged foods	0.2
Bread, cakes, etc.	0.1
Fats	0.1
Poultry	0.1
Cheese	0.1

Source: Roy 1976.

especially if the food is prepacked, except for some packages which are damaged in handling. Perishable food may have to be discarded if kept for too long or if returned by retailers under sale or return agreements. Fruit and vegetables are the foodstuffs most likely to suffer loss at the wholesaling stage but, even for these, total losses are probably below 1 percent of the supply.

At the retail stage, too, it appears that losses and wastage are quite small and do not generally exceed about 0.5 percent of the retailer's total supplies. Efficient retailers obviously take steps to keep their profits from disappearing. In supermarkets some losses will result from staff or customers knocking bottles and the like off the shelves. Some packed goods will be unacceptable to customers if damaged or dented even if the food inside is not harmed, but a competent manager will sell these cheaply or offer them to staff at cut prices. Similarly, most perishable goods are now stamped with the latest dates at which they can be sold but the competent manager will reduce prices as this date approaches. Nevertheless, some perishables will be lost by exceeding the permissible date. This is illustrated in table 29.

Small shops may handle a greater proportion of unpacked foodstuffs than do the supermarkets, especially fruit and vegetables. Greengrocers may trim and discard 5%-8% of the

Table 30. Percentage of Wastage in
Greengrocers in the United Kingdom

Cabbage, cauliflower	5–8
Loose potatoes	4–7
Citrus fruits	4
Apples	0.5

Source: Roy 1976.

product but these losses, which occur at the retail stage for the small shop, occur at the processing stage for goods sent to the supermarkets already cleaned, trimmed, and pre-packed. Some figures are shown in table 30.

Use of Private Cars on Food-related Business

One aspect of energy use in food processing and distribution that should not be overlooked—because it adds up to a significant amount—is the use of private cars on business related to the food system. This is quite apart from the use of trucks to transport food. It includes such uses as travel by sales representatives, buyers, and purchasers, of food importers and other government officials concerned with foodstuffs. It includes all use of private cars in the operation of any businesses connected with food processing and distribution, since all these uses of energy are properly chargeable to the nation's food system. Even a trip by car to the bank to pick up wages for employees of such businesses should be included. Table 19 shows that about 0.9 percent of the total energy used by the United Kingdom was used in this way in 1970 compared with 1.7 percent for actual distribution of the food. Table 20 shows that in 1970 in the United States the corresponding figures were 0.7 percent of the nation's total energy used in cars on food-related business and 1.6 percent used for actual distribution of food.

Tables 19 and 21 also show that the percentages of the nation's total energy used for processing and distributing food together (including use of cars) are 8.9 percent in the United Kingdom compared with 4.6 percent used for primary production of food, and 5.7 percent in the United States compared with 3.1 percent used for primary production of food—that is, almost double in both countries.

Consumer Shopping

There have been considerable social changes in the past thirty years in the United States and other developed countries that have altered the patterns of demand for food, the methods of processing and distributing food, and consumer shopping habits.

More homemakers today have full-time jobs and many have neither the time nor the inclination for cleaning and preparing vegetables, making cakes, and similar culinary work. The markets for convenience foods have increased rapidly and are likely to go on increasing. The annual turnover in processed foods in the United States has increased twentyfold since 1948 and it is estimated that by the 1980s half of all the foodstuffs sold will be in the form of prepared or convenience foods. The consumer in affluent societies has the money to pay the extra cost for foods of this type and is willing to do so. Yet production and distribution of such foods requires use of fossil fuel energy in amounts almost twice those needed to produce the food.

It is not only the kinds of foodstuffs demanded by the consumer that have changed: the shopping habits of the consumer have also altered considerably. Mass production has reduced the cost of domestic refrigerators and deep-freezers, and affluence has put them within reach of a majority of people. Working women and men have not much time to spare on shopping. A weekly or even monthly trip by car to a supermarket or shopping plaza, often out-of-town and often driving several miles, is the general rule. Four or five hundred cars on a Saturday morning in the parking lot of a supermarket represents use of a substantial amount of fossil fuel energy. Just how much is shown in tables 19 and 20. In the United Kingdom consumer shopping for food accounts for 2.3 percent of the total energy used by the nation, or 3.5 GJ per yr per person. In the United States consumer shopping for food accounts for 1.9 percent of the total energy used by the nation, or 6.6 GJ per yr per person. The much greater amount of energy per person used by the U.S. shopper as compared with the U.K. shopper is probably a reflection of the greater distances in the United States and also of the fact that considerably more people in the United Kingdom than in the United States still shop by public transport or on foot.

The amounts of fossil fuel energy used by the nation as a whole for consumer shopping are about half those used for actual production of food. A single example will show just how profligate in the use of energy personal shopping habits can be. A standard 0.8 kg wheat loaf has accumulated an input of 16.6 MJ of fossil fuel energy up to the time it reaches the counter of the baker's shop. Of this 16.6 MJ, about 3.3 MJ have been used to grow the wheat and 13.3 MJ to mill, transport, bake, and distribute it. Now suppose that you run out of bread suddenly and drive 1 mi in an average British car just to fetch a loaf, then you add another 8 MJ of fossil fuel energy to the 16.6 MJ already in it—a 50 percent increase. If you drive an average U.S. car, or drive a greater distance than 1 mi, then the fossil fuel energy content of the loaf by the time you get it home is correspondingly increased.

Food Preparation

Food is prepared in homes, in industrial cafeterias, in restaurants, and in public institutions such as hospitals and schools. In all of these, substantial quantities of fossil fuel energy are used. Energy-using equipment includes refrigerators and freezers; toasters, blenders, and other small appliances; cooking stoves and water heaters; waste disposal units. In recent years, as mass production has reduced prices and the working population has become more affluent, such items have become standard equipment in most houses in developed countries. The total amounts of energy thus used in the United Kingdom and United States are shown in tables 19 and 20. In the United Kingdom the total is 13.1 GJ per yr per person, which is 8.5 percent of the total fossil fuel energy used by the nation. In the United States the total is 16.5 GJ per yr per person, which is 4.8 percent of the total fossil fuel energy used by the nation.

The efficiency with which this energy is used obviously varies widely, depending on how well the equipment is designed and on how economically it is used by the home-maker or kitchen staff. Naturally, food has to be prepared and considerable amounts of energy have to be used for this purpose; but the total amounts of energy used in food preparation are considerably greater than those used for primary production of food (United Kingdom, preparation 730 MGJ, production 396 MGJ; United States, preparation 3,369 MGJ, production 2,204 MGJ). Adding together shopping, preparation, and garbage and sewage disposal, the consumer accounts for a considerable proportion of the total fossil fuel energy used in the nation's food system.

Loss and wastage of food is a very significant item at consumer level and it has been estimated that more food is lost or wasted after purchase by the homemaker or caterer than at any other stage in the food system. About 5%-10% of edible food purchased by homemakers is thrown away as kitchen or plate wastage. Estimates of the actual wastage in the United States for various types of food are given in table 31.

Kitchen and plate waste in restaurants and cafeterias may

Table 31. Percentage of Kitchen and Plate Waste
in Middle-Class U.S. Homes

	Food energy wasted
Meat, poultry, fish	17.7
Dairy produce	2.9
Bread and cereal products	4.7
Fats and oils	8.8
Vegetables and fruit	5.5
Sugar and sweets	1.9
Eggs	3.1

Source: Adelson 1961, 1963; and Harrison 1975.

be greater, but little quantitative information is available. What there is comes from World War II when economy of use of food was a national interest. At that time it was estimated that about 5%-8% of total food supply was wasted in British and U.S. Army catering and as much as 17% in U.S. student catering.

Kitchen and plate wastage varies widely in different households. Higher-income families tend to waste much more food than those with lower incomes and wastage also tends to be greater in single-person households. A considerable amount of waste is due to personal opinions on the part of consumers about what is edible and what is inedible, and these opinions are largely a matter of custom and upbringing. If the consumer can afford to pander to his own particular tastes he will do so. In the past, when people were generally less affluent, they made better and more complete use of whatever food they could obtain, and made use of many things we now discard such as bones, leaves,

Table 32. Estimated Percentage Waste of Different U.S. Commodity
Groups in Different Stages of Distribution and Use, 1943

Commodity groups	Farm (after physical production)	Transportation	Storage	Processing	Wholesale	Retail	Consumer	Total
Dairy products	17.5	0.3	...	1.0	...	0.25	1.5	20.55
Meat, poultry, and fish	1.5	0.3	0.5	2.5	1.0	1.5	7.0	14.30
Eggs	1.0	1.0	0.5	...	0.25	0.25	1.0	4.00
Potatoes	7.0	1.0	5.0	1.0	1.0	3.0	10.0	28.00
Dry legumes and nuts	9.0	...	5.0	34.0	...	0.25	2.0	50.25
Tomatoes and citrus fruits	7.0	3.0	2.0	5.0	2.0	8.0	6.0	33.00
Leafy, green, and yellow vegetables	12.5	3.0	1.0	5.0	2.0	7.0	12.5	43.00
Other vegetables	8.0	2.0	1.0	5.0	1.0	4.0	8.0	29.00
Deciduous fruits	8.0	3.0	1.0	3.0	1.0	7.0	3.0	26.00
Cereals and flour	13.0	...	4.0	14.0	1.5	1.5	5.0	39.00
Sugar and syrup	1.0	...	...	1.0	...	...	2.0	4.00
Butter and fats	1.0	...	...	0.5	...	...	5.0	6.50
Coffee, tea, spices, and chocolate	...	...	1.0	1.0	...	...	5.0	7.00
All foods*	9.1	0.9	1.5	4.3	0.8	2.4	4.75	23.70

Source: Kling 1943.
*The significance of these figures should be given very serious thought. They imply that in developed countries such as the United States and United Kingdom about 25 percent of the total food produced by the nation is wasted, which means that 25 percent of the fossil fuel energy put into the nation's food systems produces no food energy at all. Eating oil may well be justified but pouring it down the drain certainly is not.

and offal. It is interesting to note that wastage of beef was three times greater during the 1973 beef shortage in the United States than after it because people bought unfamiliar cuts of meat and then rejected more of them.

Loss of metabolically utilizable food energy can also occur during preparation and cooking. The extent to which nutritive value is lost depends very much on the skill of the cook. In preparation, for example, extensive peeling rather than washing or scraping of vegetables can result in loss. Fruit and vegetables are very prone to loss of nutritive value during cooking. However, one of the main sources of wastage of food energy in home kitchens is discarded fats and juices from cooked meat or fish. Beef loses about 24 percent of its fat content during roasting and mutton loses as much as 54 percent.

All losses and wastages in food preparation and consumption represent wastage of irreplaceable fossil fuel energy because everything that is wasted has acquired a certain fossil fuel energy input. Such losses and wastages can, as we have seen, occur at all stages from farm to house. Individual losses at each stage may be small but together they can add up to substantial losses of some types of foodstuffs. This is illustrated by table 32, which shows a survey of the wastage and loss of various foodstuffs at different stages of processing, distribution, and preparation, and which was prepared by the U.S. Food Distribution Administration during World War II. The object, at that time, was to illustrate the need to economize on food production. The survey says, "More food is wasted than is consumed by our Armed Forces and lend-lease shipments. Waste is much greater than any feasible increase of food production in 1943 or 1944. Every bit of food which is wasted is the equivalent of so much production. Conservation of only a portion could probably add more to the nation's fuel supply than any other program." This is still substantially true. Greatly increased agricultural production, as a result of massive input of fossil fuel energy, and consumer affluence have together removed the pressures to economize in food production but the figures in table 32 can still be taken as a warning against the time when the fossil fuel starts to run out.

Other Energy Expenditures

Garbage and Sewage Disposal

Fossil fuel energy used in these operations belongs with the nation's food system. It has been estimated that 12 percent of all trucks in the United States are engaged in garbage disposal. Sewage treatment in developed countries is a complex technology utilizing considerable amounts of energy.

Food-related Buildings

A use of energy which must be included in the energy budget for the nation's food system as a whole is construction and maintenance of food shops, supermarkets, warehouses, restaurants, and all other buildings, the primary function of which is to deal with food.

Conclusion

Enough has been said so far to indicate the large amounts of fossil fuel energy which are used in the total system of food production, processing, distribution and preparation. However, the information in figures 10, 11, and 12 are worth considering here. Figure 10 shows the energy output:input ratios for the total U.S. food system for past years. The energy output:input ratio is still decreasing but not so rapidly as before.

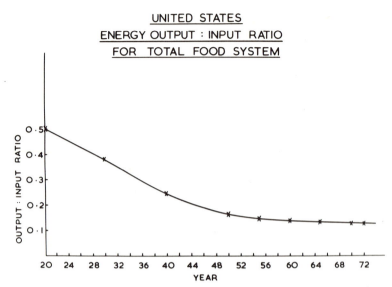

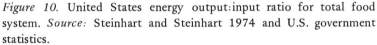

Figure 10. United States energy output:input ratio for total food system. *Source:* Steinhart and Steinhart 1974 and U.S. government statistics.

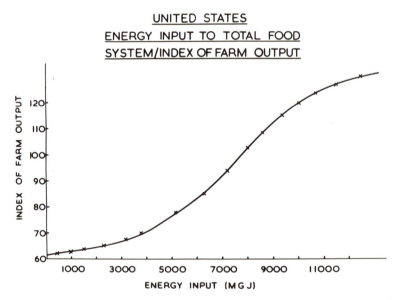

Figure 11. United States energy input to total food system/index of farm output. *Source:* Steinhart and Steinhart 1974 and U.S. government statistics.

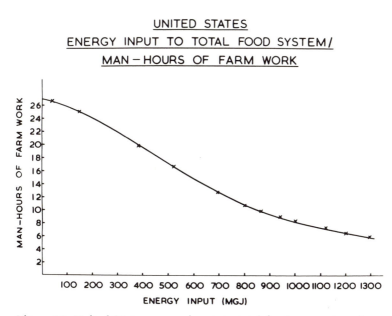

Figure 12. United States energy input to total food system/man-hours of farm work. *Source:* Steinhart and Steinhart 1974 and U.S. government statistics.

Figure 11 shows the fossil fuel energy put into the total U.S. food system plotted against the index of farm output. This indicates that the use of fossil fuel energy in the total food system is outstripping the increase in amount of actual food produced which it brings about.

Figure 12 shows the fossil fuel energy put into the total U.S. food system plotted against the number of man-hours worked on farms, and shows dramatically how energy has been used to replace labor in the fields although not necessarily labor in the towns on food processing, distribution, and preparation.

CHAPTER FOUR

Possible Ways of Saving Energy: General Considerations

For each man, woman, and child in the United States, about 30 MJ of fossil fuel energy (about 0.2 gal of oil) are used each day to produce food and a further 132 MJ of fossil fuel energy (about 0.87 gal of oil) each day to process, distribute, and prepare that food for consumption. This represents a use for primary agricultural production of about 3.1 percent of the total fossil fuel energy used by the nation for all purposes and a use for food processing, distribution, and preparation of about 14 percent of that total. In the United Kingdom, the corresponding figures are 19 MJ of fossil fuel energy (about 0.12 gal of oil) per day per head of population for primary agricultural production and 96 MJ of fossil fuel energy (about 0.63 gal of oil) per day per head of population for processing, distributing, and preparing of food, representing respectively 4.6 percent of the nation's total use of fossil fuel energy for primary agricultural production and about 23 percent of that total for processing, distribution, and preparation of food.

Since world resources of fossil fuels are limited, it is pertinent to consider what economies might be made in the massive amounts of these fuels which are currently used in the food systems of developed countries. We must eat oil in order to feed our growing populations adequately but we cannot go on eating oil indefinitely at the current rates. Because we are so dependent on fossil fuels for our sustenance we should, if we have any concern for our descendants and for the future of the human race, plan to eke them out as long as possible. Substantial savings of energy might be made at various points in the food system by avoiding waste of foodstuffs that have already accumulated a substantial fossil fuel energy content; or by not producing foodstuffs, or not using food processing techniques that are highly energy-demanding and for which the energy output:input ratios are small.

The desirability of making such savings is unequivocal, provided that the total amount of food available is not reduced; the problem is how to achieve these savings. Economies in energy use will not be made voluntarily unless it is demonstrated to the person asked to make a particular energy economy that it is financially advantageous for him to make it. Fossil fuel energy is still relatively cheap and certainly much cheaper per unit of energy output than manpower or animal power. Thus a change in a method of production, processing, distribution, or preparation of a particular food that would demonstrably save fossil fuel energy might result in increased costs. Possibly in a country such as the United States, in which the economic forces of the market are allowed to operate without hindrance, the food system has already optimized itself financially. The amounts of wastage that occur in the food systems of such countries may represent an economic optimum which there are no financial incentives to reduce. Wastage at all stages of the food system may occur simply because disposal is the cheapest option. Similarly, the costs of preventing food energy losses by installing better storage facilities, for example, may exceed the value of the food saved. Likewise, a process or operation that used little fossil fuel energy but a lot of manpower might well be much more expensive than one that used a large amount of fossil fuel energy but little manpower. It may be that the existing levels of food wastage and of utilization of fossil fuel energy in the total food system of the nation may represent the most acceptable financial balance for farmers, food processors, distributors, and consumers.

Whether or not this is true, it is obvious that if society set about changing the food system with optimization of fossil fuel energy use as the only objective, the resulting system would be very different from the present one, which aims at maximizing personal financial gain to the operator at each stage in food production, processing, and distribution. The objective of the system of production and supply of goods in a free economy, such as that of the United States, is to satisfy the tastes and preferences of consumers at costs acceptable to those consumers and sufficiently profitable to the producers and suppliers. If the goods are too expensive, the consumers will not buy them, and the producers and suppliers will have no income and will go bankrupt. If the goods are too cheap, the producers and suppliers will make no profit and will go bankrupt. The consumer aims to maximize his personal satisfaction and the supplier his personal profit. In general, in a free market system, it is the consumers' ability and willingness to purchase which stimulates production and supply and determines its nature.

The simplest economic analogy to the food system is the hooker who takes natural resources, puts in energy, and produces a commodity which commands a price determined by customer satisfaction and competition from other operators. So, in the food system of a nation such as the United States, operation of market forces has given the consumer a wide choice of foodstuffs and a great range of ways in which those foodstuffs are processed, packaged, and presented. The method for deciding how the limited resources of the nation, including those of fossil fuels, are allocated to the production and supply of different products and for determining how these products are distributed in different amounts to various consumers is not based on a national master plan but on the free exchange of generally accepted coupons called dollars.

It is not my intention here to argue the merits or demerits of such a system. If society decided that it was imperative to reduce the amount of fossil fuel energy used in the nation's food system, there would have to be considerable interference with the free market system because the optimum system for energy economy is not the optimum system for maximizing profit or for providing the lowest prices to the consumer. The system could, conceivably, be interfered with by legislation. Production of certain foodstuffs and certain types of food processing and packaging could be prohibited; gasoline could be rationed to restrict private motoring. Fossil fuel use can be altered in the nation's food system in any way which is thought to be desirable by making and enforcing the appropriate laws and regulations.

Although it would be feasible to save fossil fuels in this way, it is difficult to imagine that such action by the government would be acceptable to the public in a country like the United States. Consider what would be involved. The most controversial and difficult value judgments would be needed to weigh the importance of one type of agricultural production against another and of one type of processing against another, particularly if the fossil fuel energy contents of both were about the same. Are cake mixes more important than cornflakes, peanuts more important than soybeans, or beer more important than cola? Processing of sugar uses as much energy as processing of meat. Production of roasted coffee and cigarettes takes as much energy as production of all frozen fruits and vegetables. Beverages require more energy for production than all agricultural machinery and agricultural chemicals put together. Which should be chosen, if a choice has to be made?

Table 33. Energy Used in the United States for Producing and Processing Agricultural Products

	MGJ per yr
Sugar	114.8
Meat and meat products	116.3
Roasted coffee	9.0
Cigarettes	12.0
Frozen fruit and vegetables	27.6
Beverages	104.9
Agricultural machinery	40.8
Agricultural chemicals	63.4

Source: Hill and Erickson 1976.

There is another cogent question to be considered. If economies have to be made in the nation's use of fossil fuel energy, should these be made in the 83 percent of the nation's total energy budget which is used outside the food system rather than in the 17 percent which is used in that system to keep the nation fed? It might be argued that food is the only absolute essential and that if they have to people can do without cars, TV, washing machines, and many other manufactured goods but that they must eat every 24 hours or die.

Lin Yutang says in one of his books, "A full belly is a great thing; all else is luxury." Deciding the relative importance of food and nonfood uses of energy requires even more complex value judgments. Guns or butter? The inescapable conclusion is that any attempts to reduce the amounts of fossil fuel energy which are used in the nation's food system by direct prohibitive legislation banning certain types of food production or processing or restricting consumers' choice of what they eat would be politically unacceptable.

Nevertheless, vast amounts of an irreplaceable and limited resource are being used up and we cannot go on eating oil forever. Can nothing be done to slow down the rate at which we are using it if direct legislation is out of the question? In practice, governments constantly influence and modify consumer choice and demand, alter patterns of production and supply by indirect monetary methods. This is particularly true in the area of food since a primary responsibility of the government of any civilized country is to ensure that all its population are fed, at least to a minimum adequate standard of nutrition. So governments cause changes in the nation's food system by altering the relative availability and price of foodstuffs of different kinds and the pattern of consumer purchases by selective taxation, food subsidies, guaranteed agricultural prices, "intervention" buying, welfare payments, and other financial techniques. The idea that developed countries such as the United States really have a free economy responding without hindrance to the market forces of supply and demand is an illusion. In all such countries, no matter what the political complexions of their governments, supply and demand—especially for foodstuffs—are influenced and manipulated to an ever-increasing extent by fiscal policies. Restrictions on consumer choice that would cause sharp public reaction if attempted by direct legislation can be brought about by such indirect means. It might be possible with governmental financial measures to achieve savings in fossil fuel energy in a way that is both practicable, and acceptable to public opinion, by altering the relative costs of production and processing of different types of foodstuffs and their prices to the consumer. These methods, which affect costs and prices, are the only ones likely to succeed, since people in our present society are geared to respond to money rather than to appeals to their altruism.

If attempts are made to achieve economies in fossil fuel use by such means, the public will have to accept that government officials and legislators will make value judgments and decide how consumer choice should be influenced or even restricted. Government officials are selected and delegated by the public to make such decisions on their behalf, but it is essential that their objectives be clearly stated and fully understood.

Reduction of fossil fuel energy use must not be regarded as an end in itself without consideration of how that energy is used and the effects reduction in its use would have on the well-being of the nation or of any section of its population. The top priority is to ensure that everyone in the nation gets enough to eat. It is impossible to do this without injecting large amounts of fossil fuel energy into the food system. We must eat oil or we must starve. So, because of our complex dependence on fossil fuels and because world fuel resources are limited, our objectives should be to use them as efficiently as possible, to get the maximum energy output:input ratios, to obtain the greatest amount of food for the least amount of oil. We should encourage the most energy-efficient forms of food production, processing, distribution, and preparation, and discourage the most energy-demanding. But any measure aimed at reducing the amount of fossil fuel energy used in the nation's food system must achieve a substantial saving in energy without significantly decreasing the total amount of food available to the nation, although it may legitimately alter the range of foodstuffs available to the consumer. For example, a plan to effect economies that saved 1 MJ of fossil fuel energy with a loss of 10 MJ of food production would not be a sensible plan for the nation. On the other hand, a plan that saved 10 MJ of fossil fuel energy with a loss of only 1 MJ of food production would be worthy of consideration.

In addition, a measure for reducing fossil fuel energy use in the nation's food system should not cause substantial increase in the proportion of take-home pay that a consumer has to spend to eat adequately, although it may cause changes in that consumer's eating habits. There would be serious economic consequences for the nation if the percentage of disposable income needed for adequate nutrition rose substantially.

Further, if a plan to save energy were to cause a reduction in demand and lower prices for a particular kind of food, the economic effect on the farming community that produces the food would need to be carefully considered. Indeed, the effects of any measure for reducing fossil fuel energy use in the nation's food system should be carefully assessed before that measure is instituted.

So, any schemes for energy saving must not have unacceptably adverse effects on the total amount of food available or on the economy of the nation and the economic well-being of its people. They must be subjected to meaningful cost:benefit analysis to determine the price which has to be paid for the savings achieved.

The effects of any proposed scheme for saving energy must be assessed on the energy usage and the financial economy of the nation as a whole since a gain at one point can so easily be offset by a loss at another. Systems analysis is the only valid method of approach to the problem and is the only technique which can make reliable cost:benefit studies possible.

The public needs to know which areas of the food system are most inefficient in use of fossil fuel energy and most wasteful of energy-containing materials. In this way they can decide what alternatives would provide acceptable amounts of food energy in return for expenditures of less fossil fuel energy and how the maximum savings of fossil fuel could be achieved with the minimum reduction in total food production. The public needs this knowledge in order to call to account legislators and other officials in government departments where decisions are made behind closed doors. Political decisions are not always made on the basis of a balanced assessment of the facts but may be influenced by pressure groups or determined lobbyists with particular sectional interests. My main object here is to provide the individual with information which will enable him to form independent opinions about what should be done, or what is being done, by his government.

In outlining some of the technically feasible methods of economizing in the use of fossil fuel energy in the nation's food system, I am not going to try to assess in detail the effects of these methods on food availability and prices or on the total economy of the nation; nor am I going to suggest which of the methods are preferable or by what legislative means they should be put into effect. I do not give any corresponding list of ways in which fossil fuel economies might be made in areas not connected with the food system because this is not my area of competence. Yet it may well be that savings could be made in these nonfood areas, and I hope that other authors provide the necessary information to do so. I may, therefore, be accused of having exposed a problem without suggesting a solution, and to this I plead guilty. My aim has been to provide some of the relevant information: the decisions themselves will have to be made by the government and accepted by a consensus of the majority of the people.

   Perhaps a word needs to be said about the contention by some people that there is no need to take any action as the problem will solve itself. They argue that as fossil fuel energy becomes scarcer it will rise in price and so the most energy-demanding products and processes will be priced out of the market and, as a result, energy will be saved and what is used will be used more efficiently. They argue further that, as a consequence, the food system which optimizes profit maximization and consumer satisfaction will draw closer to the food system which optimizes fossil fuel energy use. There may be a trend in this direction but it is some-what naive to imagine that it will take place in an orderly fashion if just left to itself because organizations and indi-viduals with vested interests in the present system will vigorously oppose any changes. Rising costs of fossil fuel energy could lead to increased food prices and actual food shortages and undernourishment of the least affluent sections of the population. Better to plan now methods of saving fossil fuel energy which produce maximum benefit with minimum damage than to wait until events force panic measures which, in such circumstances, would be unlikely to be based on carefully considered and sound decisions.

CHAPTER FIVE

Possible Ways of Saving Energy: Agriculture

Primary agricultural production accounts for only 3.1 percent of the total fossil fuel energy used in the United States and 4.6 percent of the total used in the United Kingdom. It is only at this primary stage of agricultural production that input of fossil fuel energy can produce an increased output of metabolically utilizable food energy and thus give an energy output:input ratio greater than one. No subsequent processing, distribution, or preparation can increase the food energy contents of plant or animal products and, in fact, most of such operations decrease the food energy contents.

Use in agriculture and horticulture of this small proportion of the total fossil fuel energy used by the nation has been responsible for the great increases in productivity which have been achieved during the past twenty years and which have enabled the growing populations of the developed countries to be adequately fed. This high productivity must not be risked by any attempts to economize on fossil fuels;

Photo 3A. Barley attacked by fungus. (Courtesy of Imperial Chemical Industries Limited.)

farming should have the first claim on the nation's supplies of energy. If the time comes when the nation must reduce the amounts of fossil fuels that it uses then primary agri-

Photo 3B. Barley in same field treated with fungicide. (Courtesy of Imperial Chemical Industries Limited.)

cultural production should be the last thing to suffer.

Still there are opportunities for energy savings in primary agricultural production. The areas in which economies might be made should be viewed in the perspective of the very small proportion of the nation's total energy which is actually used for primary agricultural production. Economies in these areas are technically feasible but there is strong evidence that many of them would not be financially economical in the present market environment and would increase production costs and, consequently, food prices. Thus at present there is no financial incentive to the farmer to adopt many of them.

Crop Protection

Crop protection and pest control use very little fossil fuel energy and give very high energy output:input ratios. With growing populations we simply cannot allow our crops to feed insects and microorganisms, or allow weeds to compete with them for space, water, and nutrients, so crop protection must be intensified. Since fossil fuel use is insignificant here, the main problem is to develop control methods which provide maximum protection with a minimum possibility of harm to the consumer or the environment. Fortunately, great progress has been made in this direction and modern crop protection and pest control techniques involve very little risk. Large-scale misuse of older pesticides, dramatized by Rachel Carson in *Silent Spring*, were the growing pains of a new technology and will not happen again.

There is considerable evidence that pesticides are wasted because farmers or workers who do the actual spraying fail to keep their equipment in good order or do not use it in the most economical and efficient way. Savings might be achieved by a massive program of education, and this might well prove financially advantageous to farmers. The agricultural advisory and extension services of national bodies such as the U.S. Department of Agriculture are already doing considerable work in this respect.

Economical use of pesticides might also be made if there were effective and reliable early warning systems of pest and disease attacks to enable the timing of pesticide applications for maximum effect, applying them only when really necessary and then only in the minimum amounts required to give adequate control. However, in order to do this, we need to know much more of population dynamics and the ecology of pests and diseases than we do now, so it is not a practicable possibility for the near future.

Fossil fuel energy could be saved by hand spraying of pesticides rather than machine spraying but this would be hopelessly uneconomical and also, in many cases, impracticable. To spray large areas by hand in the time required would need hordes of workers, and manpower costs $6,000 per GJ whereas fossil fuel energy costs only $15 per GJ. It is precisely because it has proved so financially advantageous to him that the farmer has replaced manpower by mechanical and chemical energy. This is particularly true in weed control: replacement of manual hoeing by mechanical cultivation or use of herbicides has lowered production costs for many crops.

In some circumstances, chemical weed control may be more economical in terms of energy than mechanical methods. The example in table 34 compares mechanical weeding in a new forestry plantation with chemical weeding by the herbicide 2,4,5-T and indicates an energy saving of 1.94 GJ (13 gal of diesel fuel) per ha per yr. One chemical weeding per yr achieves satisfactory weed control whereas two mechanical weedings per yr are needed.

It may also save energy to use chemical methods of cultivation rather than mechanical methods. The example in

Table 34. Comparison of Mechanical and Chemical Weeding

	Mechanical	Chemical
Area treated per day	2.6 ha	13.0 ha
Energy used per 8-hr day by tractor	3.48 GJ	3.48 GJ
Energy used per ha	1.34 GJ	0.27 GJ
Energy in herbicide at 3.5 kg/ha	. .	0.47 GJ
Total energy for two mechanical weedings	2.68 GJ/ha	. .
Total energy for one chemical weeding	. .	0.74 GJ/ha
Annual energy saving for chemical weeding	. .	1.94 GJ/ha

Source: Green and McCulloch 1976.

table 35 compares the energy requirements for ploughing and sowing in the conventional way with clearing the ground by use of the herbicide, *paraquat,* and sowing the seed directly, the so-called direct drilling or no-tillage system of cultivation. The results indicate an energy saving of about 1.2 GJ/ha (about 8 gal of diesel fuel).

Fertilizers

Fertilizers account for 24 percent of the total fossil fuel energy used in U.S. agriculture and 38 percent of the total used in U.K. agriculture (see table 10). There are two possibilities for economizing on synthetic fertilizers, and thus on energy: green manuring and use of animal manure.

Green manuring is growing leguminous plants—which can "fix" nitrogen from the air and convert it into a form which can be used by other species—in rotation with crops and ploughing them in. Planting clover in the fall and ploughing it in 1 yr later adds about 170 kg of nitrogen per ha to the soil. In some cases legumes can be planted in between the

Table 35. Comparison of Direct Drilling
and Conventional Cultivation

Ploughing and cultivating			Direct drilling		
Operation	Fuel (l/ha)	Energy (GJ/ha)	Operation	Fuel (l/ha)	Energy (GJ/ha)
Ploughing	22.5	0.75	Spraying	1.7	0.06
Heavy cultivating	22.5	0.75	Drilling	11.2	0.38
Light harrowing	5.6	0.19	Light harrowing	5.6	0.19
Drilling	11.2	0.38	Paraquat (0.84		
			kg/ha)		0.39
Light harrowing	5.6	0.19			
Total		2.26	Total		1.02

Source: Green and McCullough 1976.

crop rows in summer and ploughed in the following spring. Thus interplanting of corn with winter vetch in August and ploughing it in in April adds about 150 kg of nitrogen per ha to the soil. On the face of it, green manuring offers possibilities of considerable energy savings since the amount of energy needed for planting the legumes would be about 0.93 GJ/ha whereas synthetic production of 150 kg of nitrogen requires 12.2 GJ. However, this sort of calculation completely ignores the economics of the proposition and also the need to get the maximum output of food from the land available. It also ignores possible effects on the agricultural system as a whole which might offset any apparent energy savings made in one limited part of the system. Rotation of crops has been practiced since medieval times and is still practiced by farmers who find it financially advantageous to do so. But cereal farmers use synthetic fertilizers precisely to eliminate the need for rotation and to grow one crop continuously (for example, corn in Illinois in the United States or barley in East Anglia in the United Kingdom).

As an illustration, let us assume that corn is grown for only 3 out of 4 yr and that the fourth yr is devoted to legumes to be ploughed in. Further, let us assume that this would give the same yield per ha as does use of synthetic fertilizers. To give the same production over 4 yr it would be necessary to grow 1.33 ha by green manuring for every 1 ha grown with synthetic fertilizers. Cultivation without fertilizer requires 19.05 GJ/ha of energy while cultivation with synthetic fertilizer requires 29.98 GJ/ha of energy. So, green manure cultivation uses 25.3 GJ and synthetic fertilizer cultivation uses 30.0 GJ for the same output if the yield per ha is assumed to be the same. This is a questionable assumption since one legume crop provides only 170 kg/ha of nitrogen whereas corn requires 125 kg/ha of nitrogen per yr. The yield of food energy from corn grown without fertilizer is 32.2 GJ/ha compared with 76.9 GJ/ha for corn grown with synthetic fertilizer. Also, the question of whether 33 percent more land is available for growing corn cannot be ignored, nor the question of what would have been the food energy content of the crops which might have been grown on it but would have to be sacrificed if it were taken for corn. The effect of using fertilizers on corn in the United States during the past 20 yr has been to release 20 M ha of land for soybean production. Yet, if unused land had to be reclaimed, cleared, drained, and irrigated to provide the extra land, how much fossil fuel energy would this require?

This example is used not to dismiss the potential of green manuring but to emphasize once again the danger of basing calculations on one aspect of the system and not on the system as a whole. The possibilities of green manuring should certainly be kept under review.

The alternative of using animal manure is also attractive at first as a means of saving fossil fuel energy because, unlike green manuring, it apparently does not involve use of extra land. One cow, nine hogs, or eighty-four chickens produce 10 t of manure, which provides 50 kg of nitrogen. Corn needs 125 kg/ha of nitrogen, or 25 t of animal manure. To haul and spread this over a radius of 1 km requires 4.1 GJ. To produce and apply 125 kg/ha of nitrogen as synthetic fertilizer requires 10.5 GJ. Although this example shows a saving in energy it completely ignores the economics. It is unrealistic to imagine that a farmer is going to haul and spread 25 t of animal manure per ha when he can apply 500 kg of clean, easy-to-handle chemical fertilizer. (In Connecticut, it is uneconomical to transport cow manure more than 3 km.)

The total amount of animal manure produced in the United States is 1.7 billion t per yt, of which over 50 percent is produced in feedlots and confined rearing situations. If all this latter 50 percent could be collected and used, it could provide 4.25 M t of nitrogen, equivalent to 345 MGJ of energy, which is not far off the total 370 MGJ of energy put into U.S. agriculture as synthetic fertilizers (see table 10). Any savings of energy by this means must remain a pipe dream until the technical problems of collecting, storage, and distribution on a massive scale can be solved and until the whole proposition can be made to look more economically attractive to the farmer. Also, it is as well to be clear what we are gaining: the manure from one cow kept on a feedlot, if used as a fertilizer to grow corn, will produce just about enough corn to feed the cow and maintain it in the feedlot.

Nevertheless, farmers should be encouraged to think about effective use of animal manures and taught how to store them properly. Most farmers regard animal wastes as a nuisance to be got rid of rather than as a resource, and often do not store them well. Efficient storage is desirable as the response from fertilizer applied in spring is double that obtained from the same amount applied in midwinter or three times that from the same amount applied in early winter.

In the United Kingdom the total amount of animal waste available from housed livestock is about 66,000 t of nitrogen from pigs, 209,000 t of nitrogen from cows, and 97,000 t of nitrogen from poultry, totaling 372,000 t of nitrogen, equivalent to 30.2 MGJ of energy. The total amount of nitrogen used in 1972 in U.K. agriculture was 932,000 t, equivalent to 75.6 MGJ of energy.

Despite the possibility of saving energy by use of green manuring or animal manure the fact is that the farmer finds chemical fertilizers easy and pleasant to handle. Who wants to "muckspread"? However, application of fertilizers is subject to the law of diminishing return. For example, the energy output:input ratio for corn fell from about nine to one for the first 50 kg/ha of nitrogen to six to one for the fourth 50 kg/ha. But in 1973 each $1 spent on fertilizer for corn produced $3.3 marginal return. As long as the farmer can obtain more than $1 return by spending $1 on chemical fertilizers, no exhortations about energy saving are going to stop him from doing it.

Machinery

The other major use of fossil fuel energy in agriculture is to power tractors and other mechanical equipment. There may be scope for improvements in design, particularly to produce implements which are more versatile, which are precisely scaled for the job they have to do, and which operate at the most efficient speeds. Equipment should make most economical use of energy-rich materials such as fertilizers and pesticides by placing them accurately in the correct amounts.

Yet, even if improved farm machinery is developed, purchasing it represents considerable capital expenditure and farmers will probably continue to use their existing equipment for some time. The best possibility for effecting energy savings is to encourage, help, and, if necessary, teach farmers how to use the machinery they have in the most economical way possible. This is a matter of good farm management and careful planning of operations. In particular, present methods of harvesting and transport use substantial amounts of energy and could be improved. Farmers might be responsive to improvements that save them money as well as saving energy.

Poorly designed or badly adjusted machinery and unskilled or careless operators cause considerable losses and consequent waste of energy in harvesting, particularly of root crops such as potatoes and beets. Food—and energy—is also lost on farms by poor storage, particularly of silage and hay.

Crop Drying

Drying of crops consumes a significant amount of fossil fuel energy, so natural drying methods should be used whenever practicable. Drying grass at high temperatures uses much more energy than production of silage or field-dried hay. Thus efficient methods of field drying should be developed, although this method might cause some reduction in corn or cereal yields. If economies in drying are contemplated, the fact that more fossil fuel energy is used for drying tobacco in the United States than is used for drying rice, peanuts, sorghum, and soybeans together should be considered in relation to the established health risks of smoking.

Animal Feedstuffs

It is reasonable to assume that the populations of developed countries will continue to demand a substantial proportion of meat in their diets and unless animal husbandry is prohibited by law they will get it. Animals can be raised on grassland, rangeland, and rough pasture that cannot produce any other kind of useful food and the energy output:input ratios for animal grazing on such land are greater than 1. However, the reason why the energy output:input ratio is comparatively good is that a lot of land is used, so the output per ha is low. Since the meat requirements of the population cannot be met entirely in this way, intensive animal and poultry raising on confined feedlots has been developed on a large scale. This type of operation has an energy output:input ratio of around 0.1 and is responsible for a very large proportion of the fossil fuel energy used in primary agricultural production in developed countries. Thus, in the United Kingdom, of the 1,116 MGJ of food energy in the nation's total production of primary plant material, 997 MGJ are fed to animals and produce only 73 MGJ as edible meat products. There is a concealed extra loss in that the large amounts of land used to grow food for animals could be used to grow crops for direct use by people or, possibly, even as sources of industrial fuel or feedstocks for chemical production. If consumers are going to insist on having meat, there is considerable incentive to find alternative feedstuffs for animals which would reduce the large fossil fuel requirements of current animal production.

One possibility is to upgrade the nutritive value of straw, 3.5 t of which are produced for every ha of small-grain cereals grown. Considerable progress has been made in the technical feasibility of doing this but the economics need more study. Forestry products such as sawdust and waste paper can also be processed to give animal food, although ink and chemicals used in the manufacture of paper have to be removed. All such materials tend to be low in nitrogen, which would have to be added with synthetic chemicals, thus reducing energy savings.

Protein for animal feedstuffs can be produced on an industrial scale by culture of microorganisms on chemical feed stocks such as hydrocarbons or methanol. The technology has been developed but it is not yet economical in energy terms because it takes about 180 MJ of fossil fuel energy to produce 1 kg of protein in this way compared with about 65 MJ per kg of protein from corn or barley. However, it does economize in use of land.

An alternative that Pirie has advocated in the United Kingdom for many years is to concentrate protein from waste vegetable materials, stalks, and leaves, including all the leaves from forest trees. Equipment to do this has been developed but there are problems in the logistics and economics of collecting the raw material and bringing it to central processing plants.

A proposition discussed by Rook (1976) in the United Kingdom is to use animal excrement as animal food—to recycle the food through the animal. Cattle excrement has a composition similar to that of cattle food and can be mixed in equal proportion with conventional feeds without adverse effect on growth. Poultry excrement is a very suitable supplementary food for ruminant animals. Human sewage can also be processed to give food suitable for animals. All

Photo 4A. Old-fashioned grain-milling equipment.

types of excreta can be used as substrates for production of protein by microorganisms, or more particularly by algae, whose photosynthetic use of solar energy is much more efficient than crop plants. There are, however, potential dangers in recycling animal or human excrement in this way because of the possible dangers of buildup and transmission of drug residues or, more seriously, of pathogenic disease organisms, and the technique is at present banned in the United States. However, there is no reason why it should not be made safe and, because of its potential for energy saving, it should be further studied.

Alternative Sources of Power

It is possible that some sources of energy might be harnessed locally by farmers to reduce their demands on

Photo 4B. Modern grain-milling equipment. (Courtesy of Cardiff Mill, Spillers Limited.)

national supplies. The technology of utilizing direct solar energy to produce electricity or to provide heating is being studied in many developed countries but is not yet practicable or economical on a large scale. It may eventually have some utility in areas with high sunshine such as the southern states of the United States but it has little future in temperate zones such as the northern states of the United States or in the United Kingdom. A pilot scheme to heat water in dairy farms in New Zealand suggested that the cost was about the same as for electricity.

Wind power has been used since primitive times to provide energy for farming operations. Modern aerodynamic technology is being applied to design highly efficient, cheap, and economical wind-powered generators. Yet even if utilizing solar or wind energy locally can be made economically attractive to the farmer compared with purchase of energy from national sources, it is unlikely to make a substantial contribution to the total energy requirements of agriculture.

Fermenting animal excrement is technologically feasible by means of anaerobic bacteria to produce gas for use as a direct fuel, as done in municipal sewage works. However, the capital cost of small-scale plants suitable for farms would be relatively high. The gas would need to be stored and purified before it could be used in internal combustion engines. If used to power mobile equipment it would have to be highly compressed into cylinders, which would require energy and expense, and might present safety hazards. The economics of such a proposition would require study and careful calculations to determine whether the usable energy produced would compensate for the energy used in construction, maintenance, and operation of the plant and all the ancilliary equipment needed to use the gas. Again, misleading conclusions may be reached by studying the effects of a scheme to save energy on one small part of the agricultural system rather than on the system as a whole. And even if the proposition were economical in terms of both money and energy, the total amount of animal excrement produced throughout the United States—if it were all collected and converted to gas—would have little impact on the nation's total use of energy. Nevertheless, the idea should be kept under review, especially in relation to the development of new technologies. (Because of the economies of scale it might be feasible to produce the gas only on very large municipal units and to mix it into national or regional gas grids; but even then the problems and expense of collection and transport of the excrement might be insuperable obstacles. One incentive to make use of animal waste is that its disposal currently presents a pollution problem, especially from intensive, confined feedlots, and the largest units of this kind might support a gasification plant.)

Farmers regard their surplus straw as an inconvenience and generally burn it because this is the cheapest thing to do with it. But an average ha of cereals yields about 3.5 t of straw, which represents an energy content of 45 GJ/ha. The energy required to gather, bale, and store this straw is only about 210 MJ/ha. About 3.8 M ha of small-grain cereals are grown annually in the United Kingdom so the straw from this has a total energy content of 170 MGJ, which is about 40 percent of the total fossil fuel energy used in U.K. agriculture, or 410 MGJ. Likewise, about 36.5 M ha of small-grain cereals are grown annually in the United States, yielding straw with a total energy content of 1,600 MGJ, which is about 73 percent of the total fossil fuel energy used in U.S. agriculture, or 2,204 MGJ.

Straw, then, is a potentially valuable national resource in energy terms. But the cost of collecting, packaging, storing, and transporting it makes its use as a source of energy uneconomical when compared with fossil fuels at their present prices. However, it can be compressed to a high density form which, weight for weight, has about half the energy content of coal. It requires only about 4 GJ/ha to dry a grain crop, so in energy terms the whole cereal crop could be dried by burning only 10 percent of the straw produced by it—if that were both practicable and financially advantageous.

Apart from the local use of compressed straw as fuel on the farm, it could be used as fuel for industrial purposes— for example, to heat steam boilers—and thus to save fossil fuel. At present, however, this is uneconomical; and it could

be argued that it is hardly worth doing anyway because
all the straw from small-grain cereals in the United States
would give only 1,600 MGJ, but the largest-sized nuclear
reactor currently available produces only about 24 MGJ
per year.

Another way in which straw might be used is to ferment
it to give methanol, which would be used as a fuel, and the
energy yield if this were done would be about 15 GJ/ha. A
full discussion of the extent to which renewable vegetable
resources might be used as feedstocks for the chemical
industry instead of irreplaceable fossil fuels is not possible
here. In summary, utilization of wastes from food production, or food processing, or actually growing crops as fuels
or for industrial feedstocks instead of for food are all possibilities. Some wastes are already used in this way, for
example, corn husks are processed to give furfural, which
is a chemical used for industrial purposes such as manufacture of polymers. Although nearly all such schemes
which have been studied by industry have proved to be
uneconomical because fossil fuels are still relatively cheap,
the possible uses of vegetable and animal wastes as sources
of energy should be constantly reviewed. If fossil fuel
prices rise substantially, these uses combined could represent
a large national saving in fossil fuels. For example, in the
United States full utilization of all vegetable and animal
waste in these ways could provide about 16,000 MGJ per
yr, which is about the same as the U.S. Energy Research and
Development Administration's target for installed nuclear
capacity by the year 2000.

A further alternative source of energy is low-grade waste
heat expelled in large amounts from power stations and
industrial installations—also a pollution problem. The only
conceivable use for such heat would be to warm greenhouses,

and there might be considerable organizational and political difficulties—as well as technical problems—in the way of such a proposition. It is, however, worth some consideration because heating greenhouses in temperate zones consumes great amounts of energy (in the United Kingdom, 25 percent of the oil used in agriculture is used for this purpose). Still, savings are more likely to come from improved design of greenhouses and more accurate control of temperature and other environmental factors than from alternative sources of heat.

Alternative Crops

None of the schemes for saving fossil fuel energy in primary agricultural production discussed so far involve radical changes in the patterns of farming production or in the consumer's choice of foodstuffs. Yet substantial savings in fossil fuel energy could be made by discontinuing production of those foods for which the energy output:input ratios are very low. The most obvious first candidates are intensively produced meat and animal products, the average energy output:input ratio for which is down around 0.1. Then there are a number of fruits and vegetables with energy output:input ratios below 1. To achieve the maximum saving of fossil fuel energy we should live entirely on a diet of cereals, which have an energy output:input ratio up around 3.0. Although this diet might reduce people's food expenses, the question remains whether anybody has any right to force them to adopt it. In 1945 Stigler demonstrated that a nutritionally adequate diet could be obtained for an annual cost of only $59.88 at that time. It consisted of 250 kg of wheat flour, 50 kg of cabbage, 6 kg of spinach, 60 kg of pancake flour, and 11 kg of pig's liver. Despite this apparent financial bargain, there were very few takers.

A more carefully considered proposition has been made for the United Kingdom by Mellanby (1975). Although the United Kingdom grows about 50 percent of its own food, Mellanby suggests that this country could be entirely self-supporting with regard to food by utilizing its 5.7 M ha of arable land, 5.7 M ha of grassland, and 8.0 M ha of rough grazing as follows: 1.6 M ha arable to produce 7 M t of wheat; 0.3 M ha arable to produce 7 M t of potatoes; 0.2 M ha arable to produce 0.5 M t of sugar from beet; 0.4 M ha arable to produce oilseed for 0.5 M t of margarine; 3 million dairy cows on 1.2 M ha of grassland to give 10 million m³ of milk; and 2 million more cows on 0.8 M ha of grassland to give 0.5 M t of butter. This output would provide every member of the population with a nutritionally balanced and sufficient diet of 12 MJ per day comprising: 400 g cereal; 400 g potatoes; 0.6 l milk; 60 g fat; and 30 g sugar. It would leave 3.2 M ha of arable land to grow food for animal and poultry production, to grow vegetables and fruit, to grow barley for beer, or to be used in any way thought desirable to add interest and variety to the basic diet. The 3.7 M ha of grassland not used for milk and butter production and the 8.0 M ha of rough grazing could all be used to produce meat. The final diet would be more than adequate in nutrition, interest, and variety.

Mellanby does not suggest that the United Kingdom could or should change overnight to this system but proposes it as an indication of what might be possible. In essence, Mellanby's scheme is based on cutting out—or drastically cutting down—intensive rearing of animals and poultry. It does not cut out meat altogether but restricts its production to grazing. It would be uneconomical in energy terms to try to eliminate meat altogether because most countries contain much land that is only fit for growing grass, and much rough natural pasture. These are useless for anything but animal husbandry since humans cannot eat grass, and animals have the very useful ability to turn it into human food. If they are not used to raise meat they do not contribute anything to human nutrition. Animal production of this kind is fairly efficient with regard to fossil fuel energy use. For example, the energy output:input ratio for range-fed beef in the United States is about 2.0 as against about 0.1 for feedlot beef, comparing favorably with corn, cereals, and soybeans.

Before any changes in the pattern of farming production and consumer choice were made to save energy, it would be necessary to study their economic effects on the farming community, on people employed in the food system, and on the economy of the nation as a whole. Energy-saving schemes which had not fully considered economic consequences could cause economic chaos, food shortages, and greatly increased food prices.

It is politically inexpedient in a free society to restrict consumer choice by law. A certain amount could be done to encourage energy-economical foodstuffs and to discourage energy-demanding foodstuffs by selective taxation and selective subsidies. Possibly the best hope is not to impose changes in eating habits on the public but to persuade them to change. The first step is to make them aware of the problem and of the need to economize on fossil fuels. Many are already very conscious of the energy output from the food they eat with respect to weight watching. There is no reason why they should not become equally conscious of the fossil fuel energy inputs. The mass media could play an active and useful part. Booklets containing the fossil fuel contents, in terms of oil equivalents, of all foods similar to those which list the calorie values could be issued. The government could make a statement of the fossil fuel content a labeling requirement for all foodstuffs. Given the right promotion, energy watching for the nation could become as popular a sport as weight watching.

Research Possibilities

There are a number of lines of research in progress in various parts of the world which, if they came to successful conclusions, could have profound effects on energy requirements of agriculture in relation to production of sufficient food to meet the needs of the population. Most of these are, at present, only at the stage of laboratory investigations and have a long way to go before they have any practical utility. Yet because of their potential for making substantial savings in fossil fuel energy requirements possible, these investigations should be given adequate government support.

Fertilizers

Production of fertilizers accounts for a considerable proportion of the total energy put into primary agricultural production, particularly nitrogenous fertilizers. There is plenty of nitrogen in the atmosphere but it requires large amounts of fossil fuel energy to convert it, by present methods of industrial production, into a form for use by plants. Leguminous plants such as peas and beans can carry out this conversion naturally and so make direct use of atmospheric nitrogen. Their ability to do this is the basis of green manuring, in which a leguminous crop is grown in rotation and ploughed in to provide nitrogen for a subsequent cereal crop. They can do it because they have microorganisms (*Rhizobium*) which live symbiotically on their roots and which have the ability to "fix" nitrogen from the air. If mutant strains of these microorganisms could be produced which retained their nitrogen-fixing ability but could live symbiotically with crop plants such as cereals, the requirements of these crops for synthetic fertilizers might be considerably reduced. Alternatively, the genetic characteristics of the microorganisms which are responsible for their nitrogen-fixing ability might be transferred by techniques of "genetic engineering" to other types of microorganisms which could live on crop plants or just separately in the soil.

The soil, in fact, contains vast numbers of nitrogen-fixing microorganisms (*Azobacter*) which fix enormous quantities of atmospheric nitrogen on a world basis and contribute greatly to the nitrogen requirements of uncultivated vegetation in the wild. If the amounts or activities of such microorganisms in the soils of arable land could be increased the needs of crops grown on these lands for synthetic fertilizers might be significantly reduced. Another possibility is that such microorganisms could be cultured on an industrial scale as an alternative to the present chemical processes for fixing atmospheric nitrogen. However, the fossil fuel energy requirements of such biochemical methods of nitrogen fixation would have to be considered carefully to establish whether they represented a real saving when compared with the chemical methods. The technology has already been established for industrial cultivation of microorganisms on hydrocarbon or methanol feedstocks to produce synthetic protein for use as an alternative to feedstuffs grown specifically for animal feeding. However, at present, the fossil fuel energy (170-200 MJ/kg) needed to produce the synthetic protein for animal feeding is considerably greater than that needed to produce protein in corn or barley (60-70 MJ/kg).

Solar Energy

Plants do not use solar energy very efficiently for photosynthesis. Most crop plants convert less than 1 percent of the energy in the sunlight that falls on them to metabolically usable energy in carbon compounds. Given sufficient water, light, and nutrients the limiting factor to photosynthesis appears to be the actual concentration of carbon dioxide in the air and the rate at which the plant is physically able to take it up. Plants have to process enormous quantities of air to obtain the carbon dioxide they need. One ha of corn has to extract the carbon dioxide from 100,000 t of air during a growing season, which means that each m^2 of foliage must deal with about 1.5 m^3 of air every day. Local depletions of carbon dioxide may occur, especially in dense stands of crops in still weather, and cause photosynthesis to cease. The assimilation rate of carbon dioxide into the photosynthesis cycle is limited by its rate of entry through the leaf stomata and across various membranes, by its solubility in cell fluids, and by its concentration near the chlorophyll. The possibilities of improving the plant's ability to utilize carbon dioxide by affecting any of these factors are being investigated.

Even given enough water, nutrients, and carbon dioxide, a limiting factor to photosynthesis may be the ability of the plant to use light to a maximum efficiency, especially strong light. (Anything that could improve this would have considerable significance for the Third World countries, many of which are in tropical areas.) Light is harvested by leaves by the chlorophyll a/b protein in the chloroplast membrane and the energy is transferred to the photosynthetic enzyme system by grana which move across that membrane and pick up and act as carriers of the energy. What happens in most plants is that the grana "pile up" in the chloroplast membrane system so that the energy is not carried into the photosynthetic system as fast as it could be used. Normally about 200 grana are stacked in each chloroplast membrane. Bright sunlight excites a chlorophyll molecule about 10 times per sec, so if the turnover rate could be increased so that there were only 20 grana stacked at any time, the rate at which energy was transported (200 units/sec) into the photosynthetic enzyme system would match the maximum rate at which that system could use it, which is known to be about 200 units/sec. This is a challenge to the scientists.

Plants also vary in the efficiency with which they use the carbon dioxide which is actually assimilated into the photosynthetic cycle. Some of it is not converted to metabolically useful carbon compounds but is returned to the atmosphere through the process of photorespiration. Possibly this could be influenced by means of applied chemicals. Many subtropical plants, particularly sugarcane, utilize a photosynthetic cycle (the 4-carbon pathway) which is inherently more efficient than that used by most temperate plants (the 3-carbon pathway). Introducing the 4-carbon pathway into temperate plants, particularly cereals, is a problem for plant breeders. There are wild plants in temperate zones that do use this pathway: for example, a U.K. grass, Spartina Towsendii, which might be used as plant-breeding stock.

Plant Breeding

Another way to increase the photosynthetic efficiency of food production would be to divert as much of the energy of the carbon compounds which are actually formed by photosynthesis into production by the plants of those growth types which are most valuable to us for food. For cereals, this would mean reproductive growth to produce seed rather than vegetative growth. For root crops it would mean storage in roots and tubers rather than top growth. For vegetables it would mean production of leaves rather than flowers. Obviously a balance has to be maintained to ensure than the plant can thrive, but there is already considerable evidence that the relative amounts of different types of growth can be altered by application of chemicals (plant growth regulators). Similarly, it may be possible to alter the actual nature of the carbon compound formed by photosynthesis to produce more of the most useful food products. Thus, there are already indications that applied chemicals may increase the protein content of soybeans or corn, or the sugar content of sugarcane, and the future is likely to see considerable developments in this area.

Animal Breeding

Animal breeders also have an important contribution to make. Animals are very poor converters of the food energy put into them into human food in the form of meat. Assuming that meat will remain a desirable foodstuff to the consumer, there is good reason to try to improve their energy output:input ratios by genetic selection and breeding.

All these research possibilities deserve to be pursued vigorously and extensively because of their great potential. We depend on fossil fuels because we do not know how to use solar energy more effectively and efficiently. The sun provides more energy than we would ever require if only we could trap it. The amount of solar energy falling on the earth in three days is equivalent to our total known fossil fuel reserves. All the energy needs of the United States for all purposes could be provided by the energy of sunlight falling on 6,800 m^2 of land. Thus improvements in the conversion of sunlight into food are desirable objectives. Possibly these ideas are most significant for increasing the agricultural productivity of the developing countries to feed their growing populations.

General Conclusions

The following are general conclusions about possible saving of fossil fuel energy in primary agricultural production:

1. No schemes to save energy should be allowed substantially to reduce agricultural productivity—that is, the amount of food obtained per hectare of land. To feed the population adequately is the top priority.

2. The effects of any schemes to save energy must be assessed on the total system of fossil fuel use by the nation for all purposes. Concentration on one small part of the system may demonstrate substantial economies in one area, ignoring that these might be offset by corresponding increases in energy use elsewhere in the total system.

3. The economics of any schemes to save energy must be taken into account. In a society in which most commercial decisions are based on financial considerations, it is quite unrealistic to ignore money. Fossil fuels, although irreplaceable, are at present comparatively cheap.

4. In a free society, any attempts to stop production of certain foodstuffs or to restrict consumer choice by direct prohibitive legislation is politically undesirable and the possible effects of any such action on food prices could produce unwelcome political and social repercussions. Judicious use of fiscal measures to alter the balance between various types of foodstuffs might, however, be practicable.

5. By far the best hope of achieving significant savings of energy in a practicable and acceptable way is in making the farmer more energy-conscious with advice, help, and instruction on how to save energy. All investigations have shown that there is a great difference between the economy and efficiency with which energy is used on the best-managed farms compared with average farms. Although the

cost of educational projects might be considerable, it would be public money well spent.

6. Any research that might lead to ways of utilizing solar energy should be strongly encouraged and adequately financed, preferably on the scale of space research, since feeding the population might reasonably be considered as important as discovering whether there is life on Mars. The sun is a free, inexhaustible source of energy if we can find out how to use it, or how to make plants use it better for us.

CHAPTER SIX

Possible Ways of Saving Energy: Food Processing, Distribution, and Preparation

In the United States, 3.1 percent of the nation's total use of fossil fuel energy goes into primary agricultural production and 13.8 percent into processing, distribution, and preparation of food, and into other food-related operations. The corresponding figures for the United Kingdom are 4.6 percent and 22.8 percent, respectively. On the face of it, it would seem that there ought to be more opportunities to economize in the uses of energy in the food system after the food leaves the farm than in uses of energy on the farm itself. Also, fossil fuel energy put into growing crops and raising animals produces some return, albeit with widely differing efficiencies, in the form of metabolically utilizable food energy, whereas energy put into the postfarm food system cannot increase the amount of food energy available to the population and, in fact, decreases it considerably because of wastage.

The comparatively small percentage of the total energy used by the nation which goes into primary agricultural production is used very efficiently for growing crops, considerably less efficiently for raising animals, but much more efficiently that many other ways in which the nation uses energy; above all, its use is essential for feeding the population. We have examined a number of specific ways in which this small amount of energy used in primary agricultural production could be reduced still further; however, it is more difficult to identify the specific ways in which energy might be saved in the postfarm food system. Although there are many individual farms and individual farmers, the basic methods of agriculture of all types can be defined in terms of a manageable number of operations. Moreover, the farming community is a reasonably well-identified and well-organized section of the nation which the government can advise and influence through the agricultural advisory and extension services.

The national system of food processing and distribution, on the other hand, presents a bewildering array of large and small individual businesses carrying out an enormous diversity of operations. There is little cooperative organization or contact between these businesses and, in most cases, insufficient direct contact with government advisers. There is a U.S. Department of Agriculture, but no U.S. department of food processing, distribution, and preparation to formulate and propagate unified policies, or to take a national view of the total system, and suggest strategies for energy economy. Food preparation is even more complex and unorganized because it involves vast numbers of individual cafeterias, restaurants, and, finally, the behavior of individual homemakers.

Although this is not my area of competence, I have been able to identify instances of excessive energy use in food distribution, processing, and preparation, which ought to be very seriously considered by the governments of all developed countries. Indeed, it might be in their national interest to set up specific organizations for examining all aspects of their postfarm food systems.

Most of the ways for saving energy in primary agricultural production, provided they were made financially attractive to farmers, would have very little effect on the range of foodstuffs available, the eating habits of the nation, or the consumer's freedom and variety of choice. Many economies in energy use in food processing, distribution, and preparation would almost certainly affect one or all of these things. In an affluent democratic country such as the United States, individual maximization of profit and consumer sovereignty are the two major driving principles. The great economist Adam Smith said, in the eighteenth century, that the motivation of each person's actions is his own self-interest. A totalitarian government can make people conform; for a democratic government the only possibility is to convince a majority of the people that what it wants to do is in their self-interest. So if the government has proposals for economizing in the use of energy it will have to convince the food processors and distributors and caterers and homemakers that it is in their interests to effect the suggested economies. Although people do take into account a number of other considerations, according to their opinions, tastes, and beliefs, the most common factor for judging self-interest is money. Economies in energy use will have to be shown to be financially advantageous to the processors, distributors, caterers, and homemakers—although many of them will not be. Because energy is cheap, any attempt to optimize the nation's use of it will produce a totally different system from one which is optimized on the basis of maximum financial benefit.

There is an enormous gulf to be bridged to bring the two systems into even approximate correspondence. Pareto stated the principle that any attempt to optimize any cost: benefit situation for a whole society eventually reaches a point at which an increase in gain for one individual must result in a corresponding loss for another. Government proposals aimed at optimizing cost:benefit for one resource— for example, fossil fuel—for the whole nation does not imply that cost:benefit will be optimized for each individual in that nation. This is a situation which arises when almost any action is taken by government or any legislation enacted. One of the responsibilities of government is to try to mitigate any hardship that is caused to any particular section of the community by their actions without detracting from the overall benefit to the whole nation.

For economies of energy in food processing, distribution, and preparation, there may be only two means that will succeed—assuming that prohibitive legislation is not acceptable. The first is to use fiscal and taxation methods to bring those things which are most energy-saving into line with those things which are most financially advantageous to the individual concerned—that is, to make the price of a foodstuff proportional to the amount of energy which has been used in its production. The second is to use the mass media and the educational establishments in a national campaign to make the nation energy-conscious and to bring home to the community that economies now are the only way to ensure the future nourishment of the nation, and of their descendants in particular, since this concept might influence to some extent their thinking about their immediate self-interest. (Do you care whether your grandchildren and great-grandchildren get enough to eat?) This needs to be coupled with the formation of a coordinated postfarm food advisory and extension service incorporating the various existing advisory services in a national plan.

Food Processing

The technology of food processing was originally developed to deal with perishable foodstuffs such as fruit and meat, and had its origins in rural practices such as the salting of beef, smoking of ham, or clamping of root crops. For foodstuffs of this type it is a necessary technology in order to avoid wastage and hazard to health. In modern times, food processing has gone far beyond what is needed to present food to the consumer in a wholesome condition. Today's homemakers—who are often breadwinners too—look for ways to save time on food preparation especially on chores such as scraping vegetables or making soup. So there has been a growing demand for ready-prepared foods. The increased sophistication of food processing is probably caused less by consumer demand than by the food processors' desire to give as much added value as possible to basic foodstuffs in order to increase their profits. The competition and drive of the processed food industry, fully exploiting modern advertising methods, has created a market for many products.

In an affluent society a wide variety of choice of foods should be made available to the consumer. But in view of the need to conserve energy, the question is whether it has gone too far. Should attempts be made to discourage the public from buying those processed foods which have used the greatest amounts of energy in their production? How many of them would really be missed? Would their disappearance from the supermarket shelves really make the public feel that their freedom of choice had been restricted? Would their standards of living really be diminished? It would be unacceptable in a democracy for a government to ban, for example, the eating of meat, but not necessarily unacceptable for them to try to direct consumer choice in energy-saving directions.

In a country such as the United States the objective of economic activity is to transform available resources into new products of greater value. In the processed food industry, a chocolate cookie, for example, started off a few years ago as a plain cookie coated with chocolate but developed from that into various offerings with multiple layers of marzipan, caramel, jam, cream, and so on, decorated with fancy bits and pieces and wrapped in an eye-catching way. This process has increased the average added value and price of chocolate cookies about threefold without any significant change in nutritional value but with the use of a considerably greater amount of fossil fuel energy. Hundreds of similar examples could be quoted in which the only justification for the particular type of food processing or fabrication is to make money by strident selling in a highly competitive market.

Surveys have shown a tremendous range of variations in the energy-efficiency of food-processing operations. At one extreme are processing organizations that not only use, but try to develop, new energy-saving techniques, whose equipment is designed to conserve and recycle heat energy, and to make economical use of electricity, and whose operations are managed and supervised in such a way that waste of energy is reduced to a minimum. At the other extreme are processors who carry out antiquated energy-demanding processes on equipment that is poorly designed and not energy-conserving (for example, because of inadequate insulation), and run without attention to whether energy is being wasted or not (for example, ovens left on when not in use).

It might seem that rising energy costs would cause firms that waste energy to become less competitive and go out of business. This is not so—as long as the consumer is willing and able to pay for what he wants or what he has been led by persuasive advertising to think he wants. Although the cost of energy has been rising during recent years, the food processing industry has made no serious attempt to economize in energy use. Instead, it has passed the price increases right on to the consumer, and the consumer has paid them.

Furthermore, food scientists and technologists are devising more energy-efficient ways of preserving and processing food, but it is naive to believe that these methods will be welcomed and adopted by the processing industries. There is a very large capital investment in present methods of food processing which will result in opposition to innovation by many processors.

The food and drink processing industries are the fourth largest users of energy in the country: in the United States they use 3.4 percent of all the energy used by the nation, and in the United Kingdom, 6.3 percent. There are extensive opportunities for economizing on energy within these industries. Research by food scientists and technologists to discover and develop energy-saving ways of preserving and processing food should be encouraged and, if desirable, government subsidized. Expert advice should be made available to processors on new types of machinery, and since processors may be reluctant to spend substantial amounts of money and effort now to make energy savings in the future, government grants or other assistance for this purpose may be necessary.

I regret that experience of the way people are motivated leads me to the conclusion that the only way fossil fuel energy used in food processing can be substantially reduced is if the public refuses to pay inflated prices for processed foods that have been dressed up to appeal to jaded appetites, using large amounts of energy without any increase in nutritional value compared with plainer foodstuffs; and if the public refuses to buy foodstuffs which have required high energy inputs for their fabrication—that is, for which the energy output:input ratios are low. The public must first be aware of the relative fossil fuel energy contents of the various foods offered to them, either in booklet form or on the labels of the various products. The cooperation of the mass media would be invaluable in making the public energy-conscious (although the media, and particularly TV, depend so much for their advertising revenue on advertisement of fancy goods that they would probably be reluctant to participate).

New energy-saving ways of processing foods may result in new types of food being presented to the public. However, the advertising industry has been so successful in selling to the public processed foods with high fossil fuel energy contents that it should not be beyond their competence and ingenuity to create a public desire for processed foods that can be made with a minimum of energy use. Let me not be misunderstood; I am in no way advocating that we should live on a diet of potatoes and oatmeal. I believe that it is possible to provide a varied diet and a wide range of choice, including a large variety of processed foods, and yet to use far less energy than we do at present in food preservation and processing. It is very difficult to assemble precise figures to prove this point but it is of such importance that it would justify study by a government team which could ferret out the figures. And this will happen only if the public wants it to happen and conveys the message to the food processors by the pattern of their purchases. In our consumer oriented society, the processor will adjust his markets to consumer demand, and government can assist the process by manipulating fiscal and taxation policies.

In fairness to the processing industries, whose technical achievements are remarkable, even if achieved by sometimes cavalier use of energy, it may be that processing of certain foods on a large scale is more economical in terms of energy than individual preparation by homemakers. More energy might be saved by more food processing and preparation on an industrial scale, leaving the homemaker little final preparation. Well-organized processors can probably obtain advantages of scale, can use and conserve energy more efficiently (a well-constructed large oven wastes less heat than a small oven), can collect and use waste products and by-products, and can use technology and equipment which is not available in the home. For instance, it would probably not save energy to supply consumers with raw sugarcane even though the industrial processing of sugar requires 24.8 GJ/t of energy, equivalent to an energy output:input ratio of 0.65.

The solution to the problem of reducing fossil fuel energy consumption in food processing is not necessarily to make the homemakers prepare their own vegetables or boil down bones for soup. If the range of processed foods available is not to be altered, it may be that their present methods of production are the best from an energy viewpoint. This emphasizes my contention that only a systems analysis study of the food systems as a whole can achieve meaningful results. We have to be very careful that apparent economies of energy in one part of the system are not more than offset by increased demands in some other, possibly distant, and apparently unrelated part of the system.

An area which seems to me to merit particular attention is canning. As the figures in table 22 show, canning is extremely energy-demanding and has an energy output:input ratio around 0.1. There may be a justification for canning at the production site of some perishable foods such as fruit, but the variety of products marketed in cans nowadays hardly reflects the genuine need for this type of packaging. For example, sausage rolls ready to heat are now offered in cans.

Another area that deserves attention is the multimillion dollar business of canned pet foods. The quantities of food wastage in average U.S. households (see table 31) suggests that many pets could be adequately fed from domestic scraps. Even if they cannot, pet foods could be sold in simpler containers since hygienic and health hazards are not a major consideration (despite TV advertisements of luscious steak for your dog, most pet food is made from material unfit for human consumption). Two percent of the total fossil fuel energy used by the nation goes into the canning of foodstuffs—apart from wastage of food during the canning processes.

Canning is the main user of energy in packaging foodstuffs but the whole system needs study from an energy use viewpoint. Packaging accounts for 36 percent of the total energy used in food processing in the United States and 23 percent of the total energy used in food processing in the United Kingdom—that is, 1.2 percent of the total U.S. use of energy and 1.4 percent of the total U.K. use of energy. Much packaging is motivated by advertisement and marketing rather than by hygiene. (I doubt if health risks were greater when cookies were weighed out by the grocer from a large tin or when apples were sold loose rather than prepacked in polyethylene bags.)

Much packaging is also motivated by the demands from the supermarkets to the food processors to produce ready-packed goods because this reduces their handling and labor costs. It takes time—which costs money—if a store assistant has to weigh goods out and put them in a bag. Also, ready-packed goods facilitate display and self-service. Recently I calculated the fossil fuel energy which had gone into packaging the various foodstuffs my wife had bought at the supermarket and also the metabolically utilizable food energy in these foodstuffs. We had acquired about 80 MJ of food energy in packages which had utilized 100 MJ of fossil fuel energy to produce.

I am convinced that the only way of effecting substantial savings of energy in food processing is to make the price of all processed foods proportional to the total amount of fossil fuel energy used in their manufacture up to the time they reach the supermarket shelves so that the public tends to shift its purchases to less expensive alternatives. This is not now happening because the total cost of fossil fuel energy used in the U.S. food system is only about 15 percent of the nation's total food bill—that is, the amount spent on food by consumers. Thus energy is not the major determining factor in price. If the cost of energy increased threefold the nation's food bill would increase by 30 percent, assuming that the whole cost increase were passed on to the consumer. This would increase the percentage of disposable income which the average U.S. citizen has to spend on food from its present 18 percent only to 24 percent. The working population would then, through its trade unions, demand and get a 10 percent increase in wages, so there would still be no financial incentive—the only incentive in a money-oriented society—to make economies in fossil fuel energy use in food processing.

Food Distribution

The concentration of masses of the population into great

cities presents formidable problems in the logistics of bringing in and distributing sufficient food every day. The variety of food constantly available in city shops is a tribute to the technical efficiency with which this process is carried out. The food distributing industry makes constantly available an extensive range of foodstuffs to 250 million people across the length and breadth of the United States. To do this it consumes 1.6 percent of the total fossil fuel energy used in the United States and 1.7 percent in the United Kingdom—perhaps a moderate figure in view of what is achieved. Nevertheless, the whole food distribution system is motivated by the financial incentive of maximization of individual profit. The job of a food distributor is to move food from one place to another; his desire will be to move as much as possible as often as possible and to keep his equipment fully and continuously used. (If you own a truck as a business investment you will do everything you can to persuade people to let you move things around.) The large investment many food distributors have in transport equipment will tend to stifle innovation and to oppose the introduction of novel systems of handling and distribution of food even if these systems could be shown to economize in energy use.

It is instructive here to consider the historical development of food distribution. Agriculture and horticulture were urban inventions developed in the cities. At first these early cities relied for their food supplies on trading for food the goods they produced with hunters, food gatherers, and nomadic herdsmen. As the cities grew this source of supplies became too intermittent and unpredictable to ensure constant nutrition of the urban populations. So the deliberate cultivation of specific crops and the rearing of specific animals—the arts of horticulture and agriculture—were developed in the cities and put into operation first within the city boundaries. As city populations continued to grow, the pressures on arable land increased and it became necessary to transfer agriculture and horticulture to the countryside and to transfer workers from the cities to work on the farms. In the process, they drove out the nomadic herdsmen and took over their pastures—symbolized in Genesis by the slaying of Abel, a keeper of sheep, by Cain, a tiller of the ground. As the cities continued to expand in size and increase in population farms spread over larger distances and more complex food distribution systems had to be devised. The technology of modern transport systems and modern methods of food preservation and processing have enormously expanded the distribution chains so that food of all kinds can be transported not only throughout the United States but throughout the world. The wheel has turned almost full circle: rural populations in countries such as the United States now obtain a large proportion of their food from the cities. The farmer produces primary foodstuffs but buys a considerable amount of his own food from the town supermarket, which is served by national distributing chains. Food travels long distances from the farm to the factory then back again into the country.

Consider a typical U.S. breakfast. Orange juice from oranges grown in Florida, cornflakes from corn grown in Illinois, toast from wheat grown in Nebraska, bacon from pigs reared in the Midwest, eggs possibly produced locally, and coffee grown in South America—all coming to the consumer via the food-processing factory through a distribution network to the supermarket from which he takes it in his car, stores it in his domestic refrigerator, and prepares it in his kitchen.

Long distribution chains are advantageous to transport

companies. Purchase of a particular food from one producer by the supermarket chains and distribution through their national networks is administratively and financially attractive. As with farming, the aim has been to replace manual labor with fossil fuel energy because energy is cheap and labor is dear. But has the food distribution system become too complex? Should more locally produced food be consumed as it was before the development of modern transportation? The financial interests of the present distribution system, however, may react against use of locally grown crops. The system is maintained by fossil fuel energy, and if and when energy prices rise substantially and energy becomes scarcer, the system may begin to crack; distributors with large investments in the present system may then attempt to maintain the status quo. The social consequences of a serious breakdown in distribution of food to the massed populations in our cities makes it highly desirable for the government to plan now for a distribution system that is as economical as possible in energy use.

Apart from transport, the actual handling and presentation of foodstuffs in shops and supermarkets merits some consideration. The extensive use in supermarkets of open freezers is obviously good for the owners to encourage consumer buying but is energy-wasteful. Closed freezers adequately labeled should meet consumer needs because most shoppers know what they want to buy and the only justification for open cold displays is to encourage impulse buying. The range of foodstuffs which are now handled and presented by cold-chain methods appears to be excessive. Many of them do not need this treatment, which is purely cosmetic as the consumer has been led to believe that "freshness" is a mystical quality worth paying for. A minor point, but one which nevertheless involves some energy use, is that many supermarkets might be unnecessarily over-illuminated.

Use of Automobiles

Unless private use of automobiles is restricted or forbidden by law, it is difficult to see how any economies can be made in this area except by individuals avoiding unnecessary journeys. Use of cars for food-related business alone accounts for 0.9 percent of the total energy used by the United States and 0.7 percent of that used in the United Kingdom.

Use of private cars for shopping for food accounts for 2.3 percent of the total energy used in the United States, which is half the total energy used in all primary agricultural production. In the United Kingdom, 1.9 percent of the total energy used by the nation is for consumer food shopping. These are very high figures. The range of individual variations in the amounts of energy used in this way is even wider than in food processing and distribution, and the system is much more complex because so many more individuals are involved—effectively every family in the country. This makes the system very difficult, possibly even impossible, to analyze.

The example has already been quoted of a 0.8 kg loaf that has required 16.6 MJ of fossil fuel energy to get it into the shop, of which 3.3 MJ have been used to grow the wheat and 13.3 MJ to mill and bake it and to distribute it. A 1-mi round trip in a small car just to fetch one loaf adds 8 MJ or 50 percent, and a longer trip or larger car would add proportionately more. This is obviously an extreme, but not uncommon, example. A trip to the supermarket to load the trunk with food obviously has a much better ratio of food energy transported to energy used in its transportation. Nevertheless, 400 cars from a local area driving in to a supermarket on a Saturday and transporting food which could be delivered by one round of a van does not seem to be very economical in energy usage. Van deliveries would require people to place their orders by telephone, however, and many people like to see what they are buying and also enjoy the shopping trip. Admittedly, too, people buy things other than food on shopping trips.

Since the public would strongly resent any suggestion that its social habits should be restricted by law, the only possibility of energy economies in this area would seem to lie in individual voluntary restraint. The development of new technologies might alter the public's habits—domestic video-phones, for example, that would permit inspection of goods from a distance—but such developments and their introduction on a scale sufficient to have any effect are a long way off.

Preparation of Food

Food preparation is another system that involves every caterer and every homemaker in the country, and presents an enormous range of efficiencies in energy use; its complexity hardly permits generalization on ways in which energy might be saved. Some caterers and homemakers may be extremely economical in their use of energy while others may be very careless. Some may be very wasteful in their preparation and use of food, others may try to waste as little as possible. Caterers commonly collect waste food and table leavings and used cooking oil and either give it away or sell it so they are recycled and their fossil fuel energy content is made some further use of. As with consumer shopping the only hope of substantial savings in energy is individual voluntary restraint. The motivation for this is not likely to come until there is a substantial rise in energy prices.

A study of the energy-efficiency of domestic appliances might be rewarding. Improvements in the insulation of ovens, refrigerators, and freezers could be made but would add to the cost. The competitive nature of domestic appliance selling motivates the manufacturers to cut costs to the minimum and this may involve designs which do not represent an optimum in energy economy. The public may be more concerned to save initial outlay on initial purchases and to acquire items of domestic equipment which they are often led to believe are essential status symbols than to worry too much if their fuel bills are higher than they need be. Mostly they have no way of knowing whether the amount of fuel used by their domestic equipment is excessive since they have no standards to judge by and no technical ability to make the required investigations. A raising of the standards of design, which could be made legally enforceable just as many standards for safety are legally enforced, to include specified maximum levels of energy loss, may justify consideration by government.

Garbage Disposal

Domestic trash, including not only food waste but also packaging materials, has a large fossil fuel energy content: by the time it is thrown away, a substantial amount of fossil fuel energy has been put into it. It is at the end of the chain, so things discarded at this stage tend to constitute a greater waste of energy than things discarded at an early stage in the food system. Waste of food is a prerogative of the well-fed affluent society; a starving population does not discard anything edible.

Not only does this trash represent a waste of fossil fuel energy but substantial further amounts of energy have to be put into disposing of it—about 0.7 percent of the total energy used in the United States and 0.3 percent of that used in the United Kingdom.

Possibilities for recycling of such waste to make further use of their energy contents obviously exist but their actual achievement presents formidable problems because of the difficulties of sorting miscellaneous trash—a process which, even if it could be done efficiently, might utilize more energy than was gained from the recovered materials. Nevertheless, the possibilities should be investigated.

General Conclusions

Although food processing, distribution, and preparation and all other food-related postfarm activities consume four to five times as much of the nation's energy as primary agricultural production, the only proposals that can be made to effect substantial economies are to try to persuade all those involved in the food systems to economize voluntarily, although probably only very substantial increases in the price of energy will cause them to do so. The fact is that the U.S. public can well afford to use energy on the scale it does and will go on doing so until it can no longer afford to do so. This will, of course, happen first to the poorer sections of the community and the richer sections will maintain their present way of life, their social and eating habits, as long as they can. The resulting social and political pressures if the poorer sections of the community are actually underfed may present government with difficult problems that cannot be ignored in any cost:benefit analysis of energy use.

CHAPTER SEVEN

Feeding the World's Population

So far I have been talking here about the developed countries of the world exclusively, and especially about the United States, the most affluent of them all. We have seen that the inhabitants of the United States enjoy an adequate supply of wholesome and nourishing foods in great variety and with wide freedom of choice at prices which permit them to satisfy their food needs by spending only an average 18 percent of their disposable incomes. We have seen that this state of affairs has been made possible and is maintained only by constant injection of large amounts of fossil fuel energy into the nation's food system and that, as the population grows and the amount of arable land remains static, or even decreases, more and more fossil fuel energy will have to be used just to maintain the status quo. We have also seen that this is subject to the law of diminishing returns because, in a system of very high agricultural productivity such as that of the United States, every extra unit of fossil fuel energy put into the system produces less return in terms of metabolically utilizable food energy than the previous one, although it may still be financially advantageous to the farmer. This means that, even if supplies of fossil fuel were unlimited, there is a limit to the extent to which they can be used to offset the effects of the pressure of population growth on arable land by increasing food production. But supplies of fossil fuel are limited and irreplaceable, so that there must come a time when these supplies start to run out and it will then no longer be possible to feed the population in the way it is fed at present just by putting extra fossil fuel energy into the food system, because it will not be available in sufficient amounts. The fact that it takes four to five times as much fossil fuel energy to get the food from the farm into the mouth of the consumer as to produce it can only hasten the day of reckoning. Nevertheless, at present the U.S. population eats well by eating oil, and most people do not worry too much about tomorrow.

But what of the rest of the world? The United States contains, at the moment, about 1/18 of the world's population and it uses 1/3 of all the fossil fuel energy currently produced in the world in order to eat well, maintain a great range of industrial production, and generally to sustain its standard of living and way of life. What of the other 17/18 of the world's population, particularly those in the Third World who have neither the money to purchase fossil fuel nor the resources and equipment to use it but who are subject to the same pressures as the United States of growing populations on available arable land but, in many cases, to a much more severe extent?

Sudden, acute famines in various parts of the world which cause death by starvation on a massive scale are newsworthy and generally provoke an immediate compassionate response from the U.S. public and, through them, from their government, in the form of aid to alleviate the immediate suffering. But the fact that millions in the Third World live in a permanent and lifelong state of malnutrition is not news and attracts little attention. Let us first of all establish the facts as presented by the United Nations.

The population of the world at the moment is about 4 billion people and is increasing at the rate of approximately 2 percent per year. Every year, there are about 80 million new mouths to feed from the existing land—that is, about 1/3 the total population of the United States. Of the 4 billion people in the world about 1 billion—1/4 of the world's population—get less than 8.4 MJ per day of food energy, and this is considered to be the absolute minimum for sustained nourishment. However, the diet of many of these people, quite apart from being insufficient in total energy, is grossly deficient in protein, which is an essential requirement for health and well-being. By contrast, the average daily intake of food energy which is considered fully sufficient for an individual in the United States or the United Kingdom is 12 MJ per day. In fact, the amount of food energy in the form of a well-balanced diet that is actually purchased or made available to each individual in the United States or United Kingdom is about 13.3 MJ but a proportion of this is unconsumed because of kitchen and plate wastage. (These figures suggest that this wastage amounts to about 11 percent of the total food of the nation, which is of the same order as the proportion estimated from information from other sources in chapter 3.)

What are the results of chronic malnutrition of 1,000 million people in the world? In the individual adult it reduces the capacity for physical activity, promotes apathy, and increases susceptibility to acute and chronic infections, particularly as many of these people live in tropical areas

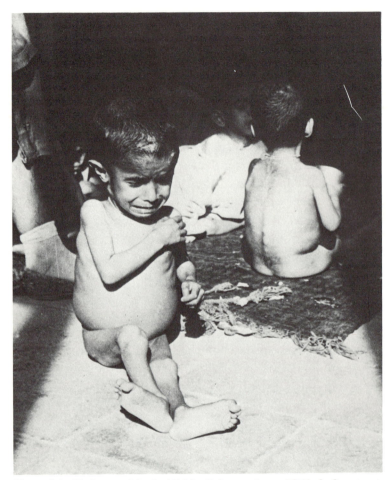

Photo 5A. Undernourished child in Teheran, Iran, 1959, before treatment in the FAO child health program. She weighed 6 kg. (Courtesy of FAO.)

where a variety of highly debilitating diseases, many carried by insect vectors, are endemic. It is difficult for the mind to grasp what this means in terms of individual human suffering. But, leaving the individual aside, it has the overall effect

Photo 5B. Three American children playing with kittens. (Courtesy of Mary E. Friedman.)

of slowing down or even halting the physical, economic, social, and political development of the populations of the countries concerned. Their reduced capacity to work impedes the production of the wealth which is needed to provide them with the resources and equipment to raise their standards of living, and they are caught in a vicious circle from which there appears to be no escape. These countries desperately need to increase both their agricultural and economic productivity.

A particularly serious and distressing aspect of malnutrition in the Third World is that, of the 1,000 million people who are estimated to be undernourished, about 300 million of them are children. In many of the Third World countries as many as 1/3 of the children die before they reach school age and the physical growth and mental develop- ment of the survivors are retarded and their ability to learn and think is impaired for the rest of their lives.

All this was said in much greater detail in a report of the Economic and Social Council to the United Nations organization ten years ago (United Nations 1968). Not only did the council analyze the problem in depth but it also proposed possible approaches to solutions and made approximate estimates of the costs of putting these into effect. At the time, this report hit the headlines and was news for two or three days until something more diverting came along to attract public attention. The actual positive action taken by the developed countries during the ten years since 1967 is negligible and has had little effect on the undernourishment of the needy 1,000 million. During that time, the world population has increased by about 800 million and the problem—and the malnutrition—have in- creased proportionately.

What, if anything, can be done about it? At present, sufficient food is produced in the world to give every person 12 MJ per day, so there is not a shortage of food but a failure of equitable distribution. This will not be true for very much longer, and total world food production will soon be insufficient adequately to nourish all the people in the world even if it were evenly shared. But the agricultural technology to produce enough food in the world to feed a population of 20 billion people exists, although the resources and will to do it do not exist. The reason why so much of the world's population is underfed is not lack of technical knowledge but social, economic, political, and religious difficulties that prevent its application. Tudge (1975) has put it this way: "In general, the world's food problems have to do with trade; equity; corruption; medieval apportionment of land; exploitation of poor countries by rich; and, within both poor and rich countries, exploitation of poor people by rich people."

I do not intend to deal with these issues in this book, but simply to discuss one or two technical possibilities that might have some potential to alleviate the malnutrition of the world. I mention the other problems to emphasize that, unless they can be overcome, there is nothing that science and technology can do to insure that all people are fed adequately.

The technology to increase the agricultural productivity of the world so that many more people can be adequately fed already exists, but it requires great amounts of fossil fuel energy. The world food problem is basically an energy problem. Given the amount of arable land we have available in the world, if we grow plants on all of this and leave those plants to rely entirely on acquiring energy from present sunshine by photosynthesis, the plants will be incapable of producing enough metabolically utilizable food energy to feed the world. So, we have to supply them with extra energy to increase the total amount of photosynthesis and the only energy we have available is the energy of past sunshine which is stored in fossil fuels and which we use to make fertilizers.

The limiting factor to the number of plants which can be grown on a given area of arable land and to the total amount of photosynthesis which they can carry out may not, however, be nitrogenous fertilizers but water. If we in the developed countries find our plants short of water we introduce irrigation schemes which utilize fossil fuel energy.

It has been estimated that 1/4 of the total land surface of the world which is sufficiently flat and has sufficient soil to support the growth of crop plants of some kind, either for direct consumption by humans or for animal feeding, is infertile because there is not enough water available in these areas. Bold schemes have been proposed such as massive industrial installations to desalinate seawater, barrage schemes to divert the rivers that flow into the Arctic Sea to irrigate the arid areas of Central Asia, and projects to tow polar icebergs to the Arabian desert. But all these schemes involve use of great amounts of fossil fuel energy.

With sufficient nutrients and water, there are two other limiting factors that may affect the total amount of photosynthesis from a given density of plants in a given area: light and carbon dioxide. There are two challenges to science in the light question. One is to make plants capable of utilizing weak light more effectively, which would enable the growing season to be extended and, therefore, the total amount of photosynthesis to be increased. This might also include attempts to make plants utilize a wider spectrum of light more effectively, since photosynthesis is confined to a narrow band of wavelengths of light. The other challenge is to make plants capable of using strong light more efficiently since the rate at which the energy of such light can be absorbed and transported into the enzyme system that actually carries out the photosynthesis process is considerably less than the rate at which that enzyme system can use it. This happens because the chlorophyll units which harvest the light "pile up" and do not move round the system fast enough.

The carbon dioxide question also presents two challenges. The first is to improve the ability of a particular stand of plants, continuously throughout the growing season, to go on taking in the very large amounts of air which they need to take in and thus feed in carbon dioxide as fast as the plants can use it. In other words, we want to avoid a situation in which photosynthesis slows down because enough carbon dioxide cannot get to the place it is needed fast enough. The other challenge in carbon dioxide utilization is that many crop plants do not retain all the carbon dioxide they take in and convert by photosynthesis to foodstuffs but throw about 1/4 of it back by the process of photorespiration. In theory, if this process could be stopped so that the plant made use of 100 percent of the carbon dioxide it took in instead of 75 percent, the total amount of vegetable matter produced in a growing season might be increased by 33 percent.

Technical aspects of the light and carbon dioxide problems have already been discussed in chapter 5 and at present there are no technological solutions to them. I discuss them again here because, in my opinion, technical discoveries which enable us to improve the efficiency of the photosynthetic process and thus the amounts of food produced from a given number of plants on a given area of land might do more to increase world food production than almost any other technical advance which could be made in this field. I suspect, also, that if solutions to these problems could be found, although application of these solutions might necessitate use of some fossil fuel energy, they might well give a very high return of metabolically utilizable food energy for a comparatively small amount of fossil fuel energy, and so enable the efficient use of some of the world's limited resources of fossil fuels. It is an area of research into which, from a world food viewpoint, the developed countries ought to be putting large amounts of money and effort.

However, even with adequate nutrients, water, light, and

an optimum rate of photosynthesis, there are other limiting factors to the amount of food that can be produced from a given area of land. The first is competition from unwanted plants for the nutrients, water, light, and carbon dioxide which are available. We deal with this problem in developed countries by use of herbicides, the production and application of which involves use of fossil fuel energy. The second factor is the need to keep the plant healthy and free from disease or to cure any infections rapidly enough to prevent significant loss of crop yields. We do this by means of fungicides, which also have a fossil fuel energy content. Finally, we need to prevent the food which has been produced by our crops from being consumed, either before or after harvest, by insects, rats, and other living organisms. We do this by using insecticides and rodenticides and by building and maintaining safe storage facilities for our harvests, and both these methods also utilize fossil fuel energy. Nevertheless, pesticides give very large increases in the metabolically utilizable food energy which can be obtained from a given area of land, either by increasing crop yields or by preventing crop losses, and are therefore an efficient way to use limited fossil fuel energy resources.

A major contribution to the food problems of Third World countries would be made if they could be provided with effective crop protection and pest control methods to a sufficient extent. The amounts of human food lost as a result of pests and diseases of both plants and animals are prodigious. An estimate of losses for the world as a whole is about 35 percent of the food actually produced, but in some Third World countries where, because of their climates the pest and disease problems are particularly acute, the actual amount of food produced is about 1/3 of what it could have been if the pests and diseases both preharvest and postharvest had been adequately controlled.

We have by no means yet reached the end of the list of factors which may reduce the amount of food which the world could produce. In areas in which insufficiency of the amount of arable land available per head of population is not the reason for inadequate food supplies for that area, the limiting factor may be the ability of the farmer to culti-vate all the land he has with the labor he has available. Nature sets a time scale and cultivation operations have to meet a deadline. In developed countries we have removed this constraint of food production by use of mechanical equip-ment such as ploughs, combine harvestors, and similar equipment, all powered by fossil fuel energy. In some areas of the world the amount of food which a farmer can produce is set by the area of land which he can sow before he has to divert his labor to weeding.

The final technical limitation to producing the maximum amount of food from the total arable land available to the people of the world is that farmers in the Third World may not be growing the most productive varieties of crops because they have not access to or cannot afford to buy the necessary seed.

Nevertheless, plant breeders have an essential part to play in producing more productive varieties of crops, but only as part of a "package deal." Reliance on new high-yielding varieties of crops alone was one of the major reasons for the failure of the so-called green revolution. A possibly even greater need is for the animal breeders to produce more productive varieties of animals or possibly to introduce hitherto unused animals for organized raising as stock, particularly animals which might be more efficient converters of energy than the food animals currently farmed.

The reason why I have discussed at some length the

technical barriers and limitations that there may be to
increasing the food supply in a particular locality is that it
is essential, before trying to improve the situation in that
locality, to identify precisely what those barriers and limitations are. It is a waste to spend a lot of time and money
trying to solve the wrong problem if, when you have obtained a solution, it cannot be applied because of some
other overriding obstacle. There may be social, economic,
political, or religious limitations the effects of which completely overshadow the technical limitations and may make
any attempts to solve the world's food problems by technological means useless. Yet in theory there are no technical
reasons why the agricultural technology of the United
States should not be applied to the Third World countries
and the agricultural productivity of these countries raised
to the levels of U.S. agriculture. But U.S. agricultural productivity depends on use of large amounts of fossil fuel energy,
so let us examine whether its extension to the whole world
is even remotely possible in energy terms.

Fossil Fuel Energy in Agriculture

The United States uses 10.8 GJ of fossil fuel energy per
yr per person for primary agricultural production. If the
assumption is made that in order to bring the agricultural
productivity of the whole world up to U.S. levels the same
quantity of fossil fuel energy per person would have to be
used, then the total energy requirement of a world of 4
billion people for primary agricultural production alone
would be 43,200 MGJ per yr. The total energy used in the
United States for all purposes is about 70,000 MGJ per yr,
which is about 1/3 of the total energy used in the world and
includes use of about 30,000 MGJ per yr of oil, which is
about 1/3 of the total oil produced each yr in the world

(18.25 x 10^9 barrels). The rest of the energy used in the United States is mainly other fossil fuels such as coal and natural gas with a comparatively small contribution from nuclear power–generated electricity and hydrodynamically–generated electricity. Oil is, of course, a key product for operation of mobile agricultural machinery and production of agrochemicals.

The total known oil reserves of the world amount to about 2,600,000 MGJ (546 x 10^9 barrels) and the potential, but as yet untapped, reserves are estimated to amount to about 9.5 million MGJ (2,000 x 10^9 barrels). If the assumption is made that about 26,000 MGJ of oil per yr put into world primary agricultural production were to raise agricultural productivity levels to something approaching U.S. standards and enable all the people in the world to be adequately fed, then if the *whole* of the known oil reserves of the world were used *for this purpose alone* it would provide a solution to the world food problem for only 100 yr, *assuming that the population remained static at 4 billion people.* But at the present population rate of increase of 2 percent per yr world population by the end of that 100 yr would have increased approximately sevenfold to about 28 billion people. This also assumes that no fossil fuel energy would be required for processing, distribution, and preparation of food—that it could be eaten as it is grown, where it is grown. This might well be true in rural areas of the Third World in which distribution would present very little problem and local renewable vegetable or animal materials such as timber or dried dung could be used for cooking, but as more and more people in Third World countries such as India and South America leave the rural areas and pack the cities— a trend not likely to be reversed—the need for complex food distribution systems will grow and, as we know from U.S.

experience, these are energy-demanding.

Of course, nobody knows precisely how much energy would need to be put into total world agriculture to increase its productivity to a level that would give everyone in the world enough to eat. The purpose of the foregoing discussion has not been to provide precise figures but to demonstrate that, even if it were technically, economically, and politically feasible to apply U.S. agricultural technology to the Third World, it is totally impracticable from the point of view of fossil fuel energy requirements.

It is important to remember that decision making in a financially oriented society such as that of the United States is based on money, not on energy. Apart from its demands for fossil fuel energy, the U.S. food system is based on large capital investment. U.S. agricultural technology is an expensive technology. Consequently, food in the United States is, by world standards, dear. The fact that the U.S. worker has to spend, on the average, only 18 percent of his disposable income in order to feed himself and his family adequately whereas the average Indian worker has to spend 66 percent of his disposable income for this purpose is not an indication that food in the United States is cheap but that the U.S. worker is relatively highly paid. In 1970, the average U.S. citizen spent about $600 out of a mean national disposable income of about $3,300 per yr on food and obtained about 13.5 MJ/day of food energy of which he actually consumed about 12 MJ/day. The average Indian citizen spent about $23 out of a mean national disposable income of $35 per yr and obtained about 8.4 MJ/day of food energy. Looked at another way, if the average Indian had had to pay U.S. prices even for the inadequate amount of food he received, it would have cost him $200—that is, six times his total income. It is salutary to realize that the $600 per person spent on food in the United States is greater than the total gross domestic product (the value of all goods produced) per head of thirty nations of the world.

So besides being energy-demanding U.S. agricultural technology is money-demanding. Its application to the Third World would require massive capital investment and a large increase in the income of the population to enable the farmers to afford to use the technology and to enable the consumer to afford to purchase the food produced by it. To illustrate this, we shall just consider the agrochemicals needed to double the food production of the Third World countries without considering possible provision of agricultural machines and equipment. These needs have been estimated (Ennis 1967) as about 100 kg/ha of fertilizers, 1,000 g/ha of pesticides, and 6 kg/ha of improved seed. The capital investment required would be of the order of $50 billion, of which about 91 percent would be for fertilizers, 8 percent for pesticides, and 1 percent for seed. In addition, about $75 billion of purchasing power would have to be made available each year by credit to farmers in the countries concerned. A new ammonia plant producing 1,000 t/day would be needed to supply increased fertilizer needs every time the world population increased by 6 million. In India, for example, this would imply 2.5 new ammonia plants of this size every year. With respect to crop protection and pest control, to double food production the Third World needs about 600,000 t of pesticides, which implies about 190 new manufacturing facilities and about 330 new formulating plants, together with about 1.1 million m^2 of adequate storage area, distributed throughout the world (Ennis 1970).

A recent study (Revelle 1976) has estimated that a total expenditure of $700 billion in capital and credit between now and 2000 A.D. would enable the whole population of the world to be adequately fed. The question is who would pay?

Nevertheless, money is an artificial convention. It determines how the natural resources of the world will be used, what products they will be turned into, how those products will be used, and how the power to determine their use will be distributed among all the individual people in the world. If an individual or a nation wants to sell all their goods and give them to the poor, there is no natural barrier to prevent them doing so. Although $700 billion between now and 2000 A.D. is a great deal of money, the estimated expenditure of the developed countries on armaments during that same period has been estimated as $8,000 billion. There is no constraint in nature which stops you from beating your swords into ploughshares if you wish to do so. The situation with regard to fossil fuel is different from that of money. No matter how noble your intentions, no matter how willing you might be to help the undernourished, you cannot give oil away if it is not there to give. So we come back to energy, and the limited and irreplaceable nature of resources of fossil fuel as the ultimate constraint.

Birth Control

A word might be said about birth control, which has been advocated by a number of people as a solution to the world's food problems. There are, without doubt, humanitarian arguments for the proposition that a woman should be able to decide for herself how many children she is called on to bear and that, if the technology is available, birth control should be accessible to all women in the world. But this is likely to be a long and slow process not just because of the money and effort required to do it but also because of traditional, economic, political, and religious opposition and objections. Family limitation is, therefore, unlikely to substantially effect the pressure of population growth on food supplies in the immediate future although it might have some mitigating effect in the long term—but by then it may be too late. Even if the present 2 percent annual increase in world population could be completely halted, we are still left with the problem of feeding 4 billion people, 1 billion of whom are already undernourished. A sudden immediate decrease in birth rate might, in fact, make the problem of the next fifty years worse since the proportion of old people in the population would rise and the number of people of an age capable of working to produce food would be decreased.

The Green Revolution

U.S. agricultural technology is based on the existence of a capital-intensive, highly technological industry to produce and service machinery and equipment and to manufacture agrochemicals; a large work force of highly trained technical people not only to operate this industry but also to apply the technology; a farming community prosperous enough to afford to use the technology and consumers who are affluent enough to be able to purchase its products; and a large input of fossil fuel energy. It is totally unsuitable for export to the Third World for many reasons, and would totally fail to meet their needs primarily because the supplies of fossil fuel energy would soon run out if used on the required scale.

The complete failure of the so-called green revolution is an outstanding example of the futility of attempting to tackle the problems of a complex system by trying to alter one aspect of that system without studying the effects of what is proposed on the system as a whole. Systems analysis is an absolutely essential technique to apply to any propositions aimed at assisting the Third World to feed its people. The green revolution is also an example of the need to define clearly the problem that you should concentrate on solving in the system you are studying, and to define the limiting factors in that system.

The green revolution began with the plant breeders' idea that if they could produce new varieties of crop plants, particularly rice, which would give substantially higher yields per ha than those varieties commonly grown in the Third World, then world food production would be dramatically increased. The farmers in those countries could grow those varieties, greater yields would be obtained, and food shortages would be, at least to some extent, ameliorated. In principle this is a worthy concept, since it is most desirable to increase the total amount of photosynthesis on a given area of land and thus to make better use of present sunshine which, unlike fossil fuels, is available at no cost in unlimited amounts.

The plant breeders did succeed in producing higher-yielding varieties, and hopes were raised. But, as any systems analyst could have predicted, the problem of increasing world food production cannot be solved by dealing with one small aspect of it. Thus substantially increased crop yields could be obtained from the new varieties only if sufficient water and sufficient fertilizer could be provided. In many areas, native crop varieties needed no irrigation at all so that if the new varieties were to be used, costly irrigation facilities would have had to be constructed. In other areas, the existing irrigation schemes would have needed extensive enlargement to provide sufficient water to enable the higher crop yields from the new varieties. It also became apparent that, in practice, the increases in crop yields that could be obtained were not substantial unless fertilizer was provided.

A further difficulty was that the new crop varieties were much more liable to be attacked by pests and diseases than many of the well-established native varieties. This, too, should have been expected since, when a species of plant is selectively bred to optimize one characteristic, for example, yield, other characteristics such as susceptibility to disease are commonly altered by the selective breeding process. So in order to achieve the promised crop yields the farmer now had to buy pesticides as well as fertilizer and expensive seed. He had no way of raising money for this except from usurious private moneylenders. All this would not have mattered too much if he had been able to sell his increased yields to the consumers at prices covering his expenses and providing him with an adequate return. But either his consumers could not afford to pay more or the farmer needed all the food for himself and his family so that he had to bear all the increased costs himself. In consequence, where the new varieties were grown in such a way as to increase yields, these extra amounts were stored in inadequately designed and contructed facilities and the rodent populations in these places increased alarmingly. So in the end the green revolution provided more food for insects and rats, very little more food for humans, and put many farmers in the Third World into severe financial straits.

Corn in Illinois

The history of corn growing in Illinois during the past fifty years provides an illuminating contrast. Until about 1935, old varieties of corn were grown and very little fertilizers or pesticides were used. Between 1935 and 1940, higher-yielding hybrid varieties of corn were introduced and rapidly brought into use by most corn farmers with the result that average yields of corn increased from about 1,800 kg/ha to about 2,700 kg/ha. From then on, synthetic fertilizers were applied on an ever-increasing scale and by 1960 average yields had risen to about 4,200 kg/ha. They then tended to flatten off, as there is a limit to the increases in yield which can be achieved by fertilizers alone. From 1960 on, effective crop protection methods for corn became available and were gradually adopted by the majority of corn farmers, and average yields rose to about 5,200 kg/ha.

At every stage, the improvements in technology cost the farmer money but he invested that money because he could sell his increased yields at prices that increased his total income. In other words, he did it because it paid him to do it. If the Illinois farmer had not been able to sell yields of 5,200 kg/ha of corn at a profit he would not have adopted any of the new agricultural technology but would have settled for 1,800 kg/ha—or gone into some other business. At present in the United States, soybean production is in this condition to some extent and, although the technical means of increasing soybean yields per ha are available, they are not fully utilized because the present market for this crop does not make it profitable for many soybean farmers to spend money on them.

So agricultural technology without money to use it is of little help to the undernourished Third World especially if extensive application of that technology were to exhaust rapidly a limited and irreplaceable supply of a natural resource—fossil fuel. What then can the developed countries do to help the hungry millions?

Help for the Third World

Firstly, we can supply expert advice to help them achieve maximum food production with the resources they have available. Why they are not now at maximum food production rates may involve systems of land tenure; cultural, social, political, or religious attitudes and prejudices; traditional ways of life and cultivational practices; or just plain ignorance. Many of these reasons will not be easily overcome as man is a conservative creature who resists change, even when it could be to his ultimate advantage.

There are two ways in which people who have the skills and knowledge to be able to provide useful help might be persuaded to go and give that help where it is most needed. Either the government could use whatever proportion of the national budget that was considered reasonable to make it financially attractive to skilled people to offer their services or the government could appeal to them to consider making some personal sacrifice for the benefit of the human race. Both methods should be used; the response will depend on the individual. (I am not detracting in any way from the substantial and valuable work done by organizations which are already concerned with the food problems of the Third World nor from the efforts of the many dedicated men and women who serve those organizations, who would be the first to agree that they could use a great deal more help because of the enormity of the problem.) If the cynics say that it is a waste of time and money and that little can actually be achieved, the experience of some pilot schemes in Indian villages and the effect that these have on the well-being of the inhabitants, prove otherwise. A vital task for skilled people from the developed countries is to train and teach enough native people in the Third World countries to do the job themselves by developing and supporting regional and national centers for research and training in agricultural technology, food science, food technology, and nutrition.

Apart from advice on how to grow crops more efficiently, how to store them safely, and to process them with minimum wastage (for example, by improved milling procedures for grain) there is great need for advice on animal husbandry. Animals are poor converters of energy but they can eat vegetation which is unsuitable for direct consumption by humans. The energy efficiency of animal production in the Third World is very much lower than in the developed countries, which themselves cannot achieve energy output:input ratios much better than 0.1 in intensive animal raising. The Third World needs advice to improve the quality of stock by selective breeding, to make more effective use of what food additives are available, to adopt—as far as is practicable—modern feeding practices, and to protect livestock from parasites and diseases.

The objective of skilled people who undertake such work must be to maximize food production in the system in the locality in which they are working by using the resources available there, not to try to import U.S. technology. The first requirement is to identify the major limiting factor to food production in the area. There may be many factors which restrict such production but there is likely to be one stumbling block that prevents modification of any of the other factors from being effective and so restricts possible courses of action. Removal of the first stumbling block may make a different factor a major impediment. But the only way to proceed is step by step. It is as if you decide that you would like to go to a drive-in movie. If you have no money, that is the major barrier which kills the whole scheme. If you acquire money, you may then find that your car has broken down but, as you now have money, you have an alternative course of action—to call a cab. If then you find that the movie parking lot is full you can, as you now have both money and transport, go to another, and so on.

Of course, advice without money is not going to solve the problem. Massive economic aid is also required, but the principle of stepwise identification of the limiting constraints needs also to be applied to determine how such aid would best be used by the developed countries to help mitigate the world food shortage. There may be considerable political obstacles since it is a sad reflection on the world in which we live that many Third World countries, if they were free to choose what economic aid they should receive, would prefer guns to food.

The agricultural technology which we offer to the Third World should aim to make maximum use of solar energy and of renewable vegetable and animal products and minimum use of fossil fuel. If technology which does depend on fossil fuel is offered it should be technology with as high as energy output:input ratio as possible. In this respect, crop protection and pest control give very large returns and the pesticide needs of the Third World should be given very thorough consideration and study.

If technology can be discovered and developed (a) that would transfer the nitrogen-fixing ability of leguminous plants to other crop plants or which would increase the natural nitrogen-fixing ability of the soil and (b) which would increase the photosynthetic efficiency of present crop plants, then these two together might do more to increase world food production than almost any other technical advance imaginable. For this reason, work on these technologies should be given priority on government research money; or, better still, the United Nations should finance large-scale research in these areas.

In suggesting technology which would enable Third World countries to make maximum use of available resources I have deliberately omitted increased use of timber, even though it is a renewable vegetable resource, because it is already used to much too great an extent. In some localities, as much as 1.5 t of wood per person are used as cooking and heating fuels. This is already producing disastrous ecological consequences as the result of extensive uncontrolled and indiscriminate felling of trees which promotes erosion of soil and the turning of the land into deserts. (Skilled advice

and help from developed countries are much needed in
management of woodland and reforestation programming.)

Table 36 shows the amounts of energy used and where
it is obtained for five Third World villages.

Table 36. Energy Use in Third World Villages (GJ/person/yr)

	Wood, animal and vegetable wastes	Fossil fuels	Human labor	Draft animals	Total
Managon, India	4.2	0.2	3.2	7.9	15.5
Peipan, China	21.1	3.6	3.2	5.3	33.2
Kilombeo, Tanzania	23.2	. .	3.2	. .	26.4
Batagawara, Nigeria	15.7	0.05	3.0	0.75	19.5
Quebradu, Bolivia	35.4	. .	3.5	10.6	49.5

Source: Makhijani 1975.

The first thing to note is that the amounts of energy used
in these Third World village food systems is not that much
less than the amounts used in the total food systems of the
United States (59 GJ/person/yr) or of the United Kingdom
(42.3 GJ/person/yr). The fact is that the energy in Third
World villages is used with appallingly low efficiencies of
conversion to useful work and consequently to metabolically
utilizable food energy. The energy output:input ratios for
these food systems are very small. For example, the output:
input ratio for a draft animal is about 0.04 compared with
0.30 for a tractor and the output:input ratio for village
cooking is about 0.05 compared with 0.25 in a well-designed
gas or electric cooking stove. This is why there is great scope

for skilled and knowledgeable advisors to make very much better use of local resources without introducing fossil fuels.

One example of technology not dependent on fossil fuel which, in my opinion, has tremendous potential for the Third World is the conversion by biological fermentation of animal or vegetable wastes into fuel gas. Prassad (1974) has discussed how this might be applied to an Indian village of 500 people with 250 cattle and 100 houses, which is typical of 60 percent of India's 5.67 million villages, which contain about 25 percent of the nation's population of 564 million. If 75 percent of the dung produced could be collected and a yield of 0.19 m^3 of fuel gas obtained from each kg of dung (a low figure in the light of known technology in this field) the gas output would be 2.4 GJ per day. At present, such villages use 1.8 GJ per day obtained from the sources indicated in table 36. But because of the nature of fuel gas it could be used much more efficiently than energy is used in such villages. Prassad estimates that this energy would be sufficient to operate ten irrigation pumps (0.72 GJ/day), five small industries (0.18 GJ/day), one light in each home (0.24 GJ/day), cooking fuel for every home (0.72 GJ/day), and miscellaneous uses (0.54 GJ/day) in each village.

The problem is, who will provide the capital and skill to set up the fermentation plants? Capital costs of such installations might be high and there may be technical problems in their installation and application. It is a challenge to engineers in developed countries to find ways in which this fossil fuel-saving technology could be made simpler and cheaper. (The rural electrification project of the Indian government is targeted to supply each village with only 0.4 GJ/day of energy—compared with the 2.4 GJ/day estimated from the fuel gas from biological wastes—and this electrification project presumably requires considerable capital and skill and, moreover, is dependent on fossil fuels.)

A spin-off of fermentation of biological waste as described above is that the fuel gas takes out only carbon from the waste and leaves the nitrogen. In a village installation of the type suggested the residue after fermentation would provide about 4.4 t per yr of nitrogen as fertilizer, which would increase the crop yields to provide an additional 320 GJ per yr of metabolically utilizable food energy for the village, or about an extra 1.7 MJ per person per day, which is about 14 percent of the minimum daily requirement of 12 MJ per person per day for adequate nutrition. An extra spin-off would be conservation of timber and consequent protection of the environment.

A further possibility is not to collect dung for fermentation to produce gas but to grow plants specifically for this purpose on areas which are not suitable for crop plants, particularly on water. The water hyacinth is a ubiquitous weed which could, if not already present, be introduced to areas of water. One ha of water hyacinth harvested and used for biological fermentation would provide 1.5 GJ per day of energy as fuel gas plus 3 t per yr of nitrogen which, when used as fertilizer, could be expected to increase crop yields to give about an extra 600 MJ per day of metabolically utilizable food energy.

It is technology of this type—and possibly others not yet discovered—which do not use fossil fuel, which the developed nations should concentrate on developing and installing with whatever money and resources they are willing to make available to help alleviate the world food shortage. But it is essential that decisions on choice of technologies should be made not on the purely cash considerations of investment appraisal which are the criteria for decision in a financially oriented society such as the United States, but on a full cost:benefit analysis in the widest sense, following a thorough systems analysis of the locality in which the technology is to be applied. Conservation of limited and irreplaceable world supplies of fossil fuel energy should weigh very heavily on the benefit side.

Global Cooperation

The concept of studying the world food system as a whole to try to optimize it not only for the benefit of the Third World but also for the benefit of the developed countries deserves consideration, especially if one of its major aims is to make most effective use of the world's resources of fossil fuels. Such a project would necessitate international cooperation on a scale and with a commitment from individual nations which has never yet been approached. Nevertheless, in due course, the nations of the world—even if their types of government and political systems are very different and currently opposed—may be forced to act together to try to solve this most urgent of the world's problems. Mass starvation is moving nearer, more or less rapidly for each nation according to its resources and affluence, but even the richest nations will not be permanently immune. The significance of present dissensions between nations may become less to these nations in the face of this common threat to them all.

One example of the global vision and cooperation that may be required is Preston's (1974) suggestion that substantial economies in fossil fuel energy could be achieved by concentrating all milk and beef production (except that from animals fed entirely on natural grassland) in the humid tropics and feeding the cattle entirely on plants which could be grown there specifically for that purpose, such as sugarcane or tapioca. Sugarcane used as a whole plant gives 20 t/ha of cattle feed whereas barley grown in temperate zones gives only about 5 t/ha. The vast areas of land in the temperate countries which are now used for growing cereals entirely for animals could be used to grow cereals sufficient to feed the whole population of the world. From a financial point of view, intensive diets for cattle prepared from sugarcane or tapioca would be about 1/5 the price of those currently made from cereals. For the sugarcane grower it would be considerably more profitable to sell beef than to sell processed sugar. The proposition would provide new employment for many people in Third World countries and would greatly increase the profitable export trade of those countries and give them the foreign exchange they need so desperately for economic and social development.

There are, of course, problems, but not necessarily insoluble ones. Production of all cereals in the temperate regions and all milk and beef in the tropics would necessitate greatly expanded and more complex worldwide distribution systems, which use fossil fuel energy. However, if as a result of removal of the energy-expensive production of animals from the developed temperate countries those countries needed to import less oil, the supertankers at present used to transport that oil might be adapted to carry milk and beef, and the overall energy balance might not be unfavorable. Also, any reduction in the amounts of oil imported by developed countries would be financially advantageous to them.

The food technologists would need to solve the problems of preservation, but most of the technology needed for this is already known. Pesticides and veterinary medicines would need to be provided on a massive scale to protect tropical cattle from the parasites and diseases to which they would be exposed there.

The loss of sugar production from sugarcane would not be a serious matter since sugar is not an essential constituent of human diet and too great a consumption of it is actually undesirable from a health viewpoint. Sugar could be replaced by synthetic sweetening agents, or some of the land in temperate countries set free from cultivation of cereals for animal feed could be used to grow sugar beet. Production of pigs and poultry, which compete directly with humans for food, would have to be drastically reduced but this might be an acceptable price to pay to relieve world hunger.

An idea was put forward by Taylor and Humpstone (1973) which might be even more esoteric but which nevertheless might repay careful study as it may have a germ of potential in it. They suggest that if greenhouses could be designed in which photosynthetic energy conversions of 10 percent could be achieved (and this is not impossible in a controlled environment) and which made maximum use of solar energy for heating so that they required little fossil fuel energy to maintain adequate temperatures, such greenhouses covering 150 million ha, or 2 percent of the total arable land in the world, would provide *both* food and fuel sufficient for 7,000 million people—1 million MGJ, or about 15 MJ/hr/person of energy of which only 0.5 MJ/hr/person is needed as metabolically utilizable food energy. This calculation assumes an average annual solar radiation intensity of 1 MJ/m^2/hr, which is about that of the sunnier part of the United States.

All the energy used by the United States in 1970 (about 70,000 MGJ) could be supplied by greenhouses covering an area of 10 million ha, which is about half the size of the state of Utah. Even in the United Kingdom, where average solar radiation is only about 0.5 MJ/m^2/hr, 10 percent of photosynthetic efficiency would provide the present average total U.K. energy consumption of about 18 MJ/hr/person from 400 m² of land per person or a total for the whole population of about 9 percent of the total land area of the United Kingdom.

Part of the crops grown would be eaten and part burnt in power stations to supply electricity. This project does not provide mobile energy, for example, for automobiles. It may be objected that it is technologically impossible or prohibitively expensive but it is probably no more so than developing and installing fast breeder atomic energy technology on a comparable scale, and certainly less so than designing and constructing a rocket to go to the moon.

Systems such as the two described above deserve careful study and cost:benefit analysis in the widest sense by the developed nations of the world. Whether they will have the vision and will to do so until hunger actually begins to bite at them is, unfortunately, doubtful.

CHAPTER EIGHT

The Final Reckoning

I hope that by now the reader appreciates the nature of the problems of use of fossil fuel energy in the nation's food system and the serious implications they may have for the future if nothing is done about them. My object has been to provide quantitative information about the rate at which energy is being used up to enable us to eat the way we do eat, and to suggest some ways in which economies might be made. I have related this to the total fossil fuel energy used by the nation but have not discussed the ways in which energy is used for nonfood purposes, or how savings might be made in these areas because I am not qualified to do so. I have drawn attention to the food problems of the world and I have mentioned the economic, social, and political considerations which affect the food system both within the United States itself and in the world as a whole and which, together with the technological considerations, make up the total system which needs to be studied in detail.

I have not attempted to analyze these economic, social, and political factors partly because I am not capable of doing so but more particularly because a full systems analysis would require the efforts of a large team of people of various skills for a considerable period in view of its intricacies and complexities. It is a job which only the government is in a position to commission, and the government is more likely to take the necessary action if there is sufficient demand from the public. I am suggesting that the public ought to make that demand.

This does not, however, take away from individual members of the nation their personal responsibility for achieving whatever economies they can in use of fossil fuel energy. Major energy savings in the food system, particularly in the areas of processing, distribution, and preparation, can be brought about only by individual action. But, it also needs to be clearly understood that whether the government takes action as a result of public demand or whether the individual takes voluntary action, the end result may be that many people will have to change their social and eating habits and their way of life. They will also have to bear the monetary costs of the tremendous amount of work which would be needed to make a comprehensive systems analysis of energy use and to implement any action which appeared desirable as a result of such a study. In order to provide each person with the motivation to take individual voluntary action or to press for government action on a national scale, the results of which would, at the very least, involve that person in some inconvenience and might call for considerable personal sacrifice, everyone in the nation needs to consider and answer for himself a number of basic questions.

Even if he thinks about the United States alone and neglects the rest of the world, some of these questions are:

Do I care whether the future inhabitants of the United States, including my own descendants, have enough to eat? Or shall I eat, drink, and be merry and let those who come after me do the best they can? Have I any right to use as much as I like of an irreplaceable, limited natural resource such as fossil fuel without any consideration for the needs of the unborn? Has any individual the right to use as much as he likes of such a resource simply because he has the money to pay for it?

If the individual is willing to look beyond the boundaries of the United States at the undernourished millions in the Third World, there are still more questions to answer:

Do I care about the human race as a whole? Am I my brother's keeper or is what happens to other people of no concern to me? Does the happy chance, over which I had no control and for which I can take no personal credit, that I was born in the United States rather than in the Third World, automatically entitle me to a larger share of the world's resources? Is it right that the United States, which contains 1/18 of the world's population, should be using up 1/3 of the present world production of irreplaceable fossil fuel energy? Do I want, as Snow has said, to watch on my TV the spectacle of millions of people in less privileged countries starving to death before my very eyes?

As I write this in February 1977 the United States has been suffering the most severe winter within living memory. This has brought home to the American people in a dramatic way the extent to which their way of life and their well-being are dependent on energy supplies and has demonstrated to them that their adequate nourishment, let alone any other necessities or luxuries of life, may be entirely at the mercy of one year's weather. The whole world is now literally living from one harvest to the next. Only four nations—the United States, Canada, Australia, and New Zealand—have a net agricultural surplus for export, and this can change dramatically in one season as when the drought of 1972 completely emptied the vast grain silos of the Midwest.

A few nights ago I watched the new U.S. president, Jimmy Carter, giving the first of his "fireside talks." He said that the United States is the only industralized nation that has no long-term energy plan and implied that he was going to try to do something about it. Any such plan must give top priority to ensuring that there will be food enough to nourish the increasing population of the nation. Lin Yutang said, "A full belly is a great thing; all else is luxury." Let us never forget this. Let us remember, too, that hunger is not confined to distant parts of the globe and to other nations, that it is not a matter of a completely well-fed United States and an undernourished Third World, but that 25 million people in the United States—that is, 1/10 of the total population—are living at poverty level. The jaws of hunger are already snapping at the underbelly of the United States and will eventually reach even those stomachs which are presently well-filled.

Where should the individual make some personal energy savings? The answer will, of course, depend on what each person thinks he could best do without. But he might like to consider the following:

1. The average American gets about 13 MJ per day of food which requires production of 22 MJ per day of vegetable food because animals are very poor converters of energy. The average Indian gets the equivalent of about 10 MJ per day of vegetable food.

2. According to Rice (1972), the total amount of fossil fuel energy used in the United States in 1970 by automobiles (not trucks or wagons, just cars) was 17,800 MGJ. The total

energy used in primary agricultural production in the United States in that year was 2,204 MGJ and the total used in the whole U.S. food system was 12,000 MGJ. Even accepting the high ratio of 6 MJ of fossil fuel energy that needs to be put into the total U.S. food system to give 1 MJ of metabolically utilizable food energy, the energy used in automobiles could, if used differently, feed about 300 million people—50 percent more than the present population of the United States. Furthermore, a United States automobile takes 300 GJ (1 t) of fossil fuel energy to produce—enough to give 50 GJ of food energy, which would feed seventeen people for 1 year.

3. Of the 13 MJ per day of food which the average American gets, he consumes only about 12 MJ. Each person wastes, on the average, 1 MJ of food each day in kitchens and on plates, and for the United States as a whole this amounts to a total wastage of about 200 million MJ per day—enough to feed another 17 million people.

4. While this waste of food is going on, the inhabitants of the United States buy about 2.5 million t per yr of processed pet foods. If the reasonable assumption is made that the metabolically utilizable food energy in these is, on the average, about 10 GJ per t, this represents a total consumption of processed food by pets in the United States of about 68,000 GJ per day of food energy, compared with a total consumption by humans of about 2.4 million GJ per day—about 3 percent. Admittedly, a large proportion of this pet food is not fit for human consumption, but one might well conclude that if the 200,000 GJ per day of kitchen and plate wastage could be fed to pets, it would supply about three times the food needs of all the pets in the nation.

Furthermore, if the reasonable assumption is made that the total amount of fossil fuel energy needed to produce, process, package, and distribute the average pet food is about 50 GJ per t, then total production accounts for 125 MGJ per yr of fossil fuel energy, which is about 1 percent of the total fossil fuel energy (about 12,000 MGJ per yr) used in the nation's food system. Even if one again accepts the present high ratio of 6 MJ of fossil fuel energy to give 1 MJ of metabolically utilizable food energy, the 125 MGJ/yr of energy used to supply pet foods could, if used in a different way, provide food for 2 million people.

It would be unfair to suggest that the United States is unique. Most of the facts given above also apply to all developed countries. Like the American, the average citizen of the United Kingdom gets about 13 MJ of food each day, eats 12 MJ, and wastes 1 MJ. According to Fears (1976), the people of the United Kingdom buy about 600,000 t per yr of processed pet foods for their pets. They drive around in cars and, although their cars are smaller and the average distances they cover are substantially less, they still use large amounts of fossil fuels for this purpose.

If the individual then turns his thoughts from what personal savings he might make in energy use to what action he should press the government to take, the immediate answer should be for government to institute a full-scale systems analysis of fossil fuel energy use by the nation. It would be foolish to try to anticipate what methods of energy economy would, as a result of such a study, promise the optimum cost: benefit. However, there are some broad general questions to be considered. Food is clearly a top priority. Essential industry must be kept going in a highly industrialized nation. But it would be pertinent to ask whether a large proportion of the goods manufactured in the United States are really essential and to ask each American whether the quality of his life and his state of well-being would be seriously diminished if he had to do without many of the luxuries he now buys. Keeping warm is an essential need, as this winter showed, but it is also reasonable to ask whether the current standards of U.S. heating are too high. Also, it takes considerably more fossil fuel energy to cool a building by 10° than to heat it by 10°, so standards of air conditioning merit attention. Use of very large amounts of fossil fuel energy on armaments and on exploration of space are contentious subjects on which opinions vary widely. The large amounts of fossil fuel used in private automobiles likewise cannot escape consideration.

I am not suggesting that individuals should be kept from using the fair rewards of their labors to pursue their individual satisfactions in their own way. Man cannot live by bread alone—but He who said that did not mean to imply that TV sets or electric golf carts are essential to a person's well-being. If the gratification of an individual's desires involve the consumption by him of an irreplaceable amount of fossil fuel energy then neither he nor the whole collection of individuals like him who constitute the nation can be allowed to use up as much as they like. There must be limits. The only way freedom *from* any evil, such as hunger, can be achieved is by individuals voluntarily giving up their freedom *to do* certain things. In fact, individuals are not, in practice, allowed to utilize all the rewards of their labors as they like because a considerable proportion of these rewards are taken by the government in taxation to spend as government thinks fit, which requires value judgments by government officials.

A very desirable objective for a comprehensive systems analysis of fossil fuel energy by the nation would be production of a list, for the guidance of the public, of the total fossil fuel energy contents of every type of commodity that is produced, similar to the one I have given for a variety of foodstuffs on page 50. How much fossil fuel energy goes into production of a TV set, a suit of clothes, a suite of furniture, a rifle, a supersonic aircraft, an atom bomb, or a Polaris missile? We know, for example, that, in the United States it takes 300 GJ to produce 1 t of automobile compared with 20 GJ to produce 1 t of bread.

If the individual thinks beyond what might be done in the United States to what might be done to alleviate the hunger of the whole world, he will conclude that the systems analysis needed and the decisions required become much more difficult, and might well call for even greater personal sacrifices from him. On an individual basis, apart from supporting relief organizations, the pressing need is for those people who have the skills and knowledge which would enable Third World populations to use their resources better and produce more food for themselves to accept the personal sacrifice of making themselves available to Third World countries, even if only for a limited period. Apart from this, the matter lies with government and it has to be decided whether it is feasible for one government, like that of the United States to tackle the problem alone, even if it got no cooperation from any other nations. If the government did go ahead, the decision would have to be made to divert a large proportion of the money and manpower currently available for scientific and technological research to those problems the solution of which might have a profound effect on world food production potential without immediately increasing fossil fuel energy demands. This might well imply a substantial reduction in research on new weapons or on space exploration or, for that matter, on production of new luxury consumer goods. But the crux of the matter is illustrated by figure 13.

Figure 13 shows results obtained by Slesser (1973) by analyzing the energy output:input ratios of 137 different

FOSSIL FUEL ENERGY INPUT TO AGRICULTURE FOR FOOD PRODUCTION

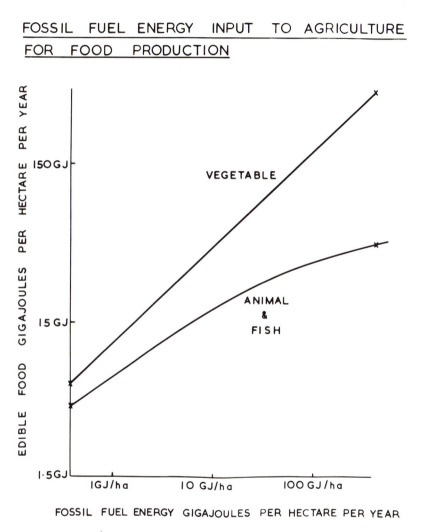

Figure 13. Fossil fuel energy input to agriculture for food production. *Source:* Slesser 1973.

systems of primary agricultural production, including production of various types of crops and raising of different kinds of animals in countries ranging from primitive agriculture to modern U.S. farming. It illustrates clearly the difference between vegetable and animal production. Within the limits of the study, extra input of fossil fuel energy into crop production continued to produce an increase in food energy output. But the law of diminishing returns is rapidly reached for animal and fish production when even substantial extra inputs of fossil fuel energy produce practically no increase in food energy output.

However, there are concealed implications which may not be immediately apparent to the nontechnical reader. The lines in figure 13 are drawn on a logarithmic scale. They consequently indicate that fossil fuel energy put into an agricultural system which is not getting very much put into it at present produces a greater relative effect on food energy output than is obtained by putting the same amount of energy into an agricultural system which is already receiving a substantial amount. A few numerical examples from figure 13 will illustrate this.

A fossil fuel energy input of 1.5 GJ/ha/yr into vegetable production produces about 16 GJ/ha/yr of food energy (these are almost exactly the energy input and output for corn grown in Nigeria). If another 10 GJ/ha/yr of fossil fuel energy were put into this vegetable production, the output of food energy would be increased to about 54 GJ/ha/yr—that is, an increase of about 38 GJ/ha/yr of food energy, or enough to feed about another nine people per ha per yr at 12 MJ of food energy per day. Ten GJ/ha/yr is almost exactly the amount of fossil fuel energy which is normally put into corn in the United States as nitrogenous fertilizer.

On the other hand, a fossil fuel energy input of 30

GJ/ha/yr into vegetable production produces about 80 GJ/ha/yr of food energy (these are almost exactly the energy inputs and outputs for corn grown in the United States). If another 10 GJ/ha/yr of fossil fuel energy were put into this vegetable production, the output of food energy would be increased to about 106 GJ/ha/yr—that is, an increase of only about 26 GJ/ha/yr of food energy, or enough to feed only about another five people per ha per yr at 12 MJ of food energy per day.

A fossil fuel energy input of 1.5 GJ/ha/yr into animal production produces about 8 GJ/ha/yr of food energy. If another 10 GJ/ha/yr of fossil fuel energy were put into this animal production, the output of food energy would be increased to about 21 GJ/ha/yr—that is, an increase of about 13 GJ/ha/yr or enough to feed about another three people per ha per yr at 12 MJ of food energy per day. Ten GJ/ha/yr is almost exactly the amount of fossil fuel energy which is normally put as concentrated animal feed into milk cows in the United Kingdom. On the other hand, a fossil fuel energy input of 30 GJ/ha/yr into animal production produces about 30 GJ/ha/yr of food energy. If another 10 GJ/ha/yr of fossil fuel energy were put into this animal production, the output of food energy would be increased to about 33 GJ/ha/yr—that is, an increase of only about 3 GJ/ha/yr of food energy, or enough to feed only about another 3/4 of a person per ha per yr at 12 MJ of food energy per day.

The conclusion is that, if a developed country such as the United States really wants to help ameliorate the hunger of the Third World countries, it should divert to those countries a substantial amount of the fertilizers and pesticides which it produces instead of allowing them to be used in domestic agriculture, and should make available to those countries a substantial proportion of the fossil fuel which it at present uses itself in order to enable them to irrigate their land and cultivate it efficiently. I am well aware that the economic, social, and political difficulties would be tremendous and that, unless skilled advisers in sufficient numbers went with the materials, it is unlikely that they would be used effectively and quite possibly that they would do no good at all. The lessons of the failure of the green revolution need to be learned: the only proposition which could help the Third World is a full "package deal" of materials, men, and money. I am not advocating any particular course of action; I am merely pointing out the inexorable implication of figure 13. I have no intention of discussing what, if anything, should in fact be done. But, if the U.S. government did decide to take action a vital question would be, Who pays? The only possible answer is the U.S. public.

It is most unlikely that a corn farmer in Illinois would voluntarily refrain from using another 50 kg/ha of fertilizer on his crop and thereby reduce the standard of living of himself and his family if you told him that by sending that 50 kg of fertilizer to India he would save a number of people from starvation. It would be quite improper to face one individual or one set of individuals in a community with a decision of that type. If there is a price to be paid, then the cost must be distributed fairly over the whole population.

So, we now come back to the question with which we began, How long can we go on eating oil? It is necessary to ask this question because world population has grown and is growing, while the amount of arable land in the world remains constant. If we had more land or a smaller population, there would be no energy problem. The Kung bushman eats well, has ample leisure, but also has 1,040 ha of land per person. The population of many regions of the world has already outgrown the capability of the arable land which they have available to supply their food needs using solar energy alone, and the situation is getting rapidly worse as world population increases by 2 percent per yr. Those regions which are not able or cannot afford to obtain and use fossil fuel energy progress steadily toward greater degrees of malnutrition. The developed countries, all of which have this problem to a greater or lesser degree, solve it temporarily by putting ever-increasing amounts of fossil fuel energy into their food systems. How long can they go on doing so? Some indication of the answer is given in figures 14 and 15.

These two figures show a compilation of information on energy output:input for primary agricultural production systems from the work of Slesser illustrated in figure 13 and from all information of this type which could be obtained from any sources to which I had access. Figure 14 shows the minimum amount of fossil fuel energy, assuming that this energy is used as efficiently as possible, which has to be put into primary crop production per head of population to give each person a totally vegetable-products diet of 12 MJ of food energy per day (the average amount each person in the United States consumes), plotted against the amount of arable land (land suitable for cultivation) available per person in the region where he lives. Figure 15 shows a similar graph of energy per person per yr needed to give a totally animal-products diet of 12 MJ of food energy per day, but plotted against the amount of agricultural land (arable land and grassland) which is available to each person.

The graphs are, once again, plotted on a logarithmic scale. From figure 14 it will be seen that the amount of energy needed to be put into crop production for each person in each yr to provide a sufficient vegetable-products diet

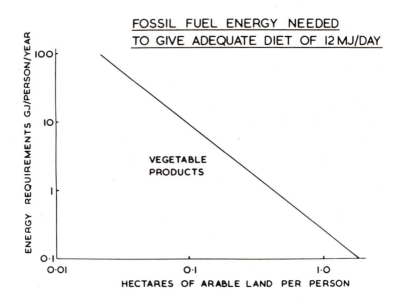

Figure 14. Fossil fuel energy needed to give adequate diet of 12 MJ/day. *Source:* Slesser 1973 and others.

increases from about 0.8 GJ/head/yr at 0.5 ha/person to about 2 GJ/head/yr at 0.25/ha/person, or increases 2.5 times as the amount of land is halved, but then increases to about 7 GJ/head/yr at 0.125/ha/person, or increases another 3.5 times as the amount of land is halved again. This is an overall increase of about nine times as you go from 0.5 ha of land per person to 0.125 ha of land per person.

But it is for a sufficient animal products diet that the figures are startling. From figure 15 it will be seen that the amount of energy needed to be put into animal production for each person in each yr to provide a sufficient animal-products diet increases from about 2 GJ/head/yr at 0.5 ha/person to about 10 GJ/head/yr at 0.25 ha/person, or increases five times as the amount of land is halved, but then increases to about 100 GJ/head/yr at 0.125 ha/person, or

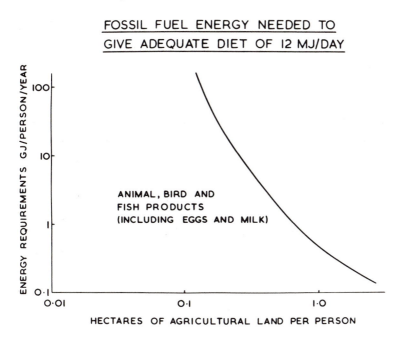

FOSSIL FUEL ENERGY NEEDED TO
GIVE ADEQUATE DIET OF 12 MJ/DAY

ANIMAL, BIRD AND
FISH PRODUCTS
(INCLUDING EGGS AND MILK)

Figure 15. Fossil fuel energy needed to give adequate diet of 12 MJ/day. *Source:* Slesser 1973 and others.

increases another ten times as the amount of land is halved again. This is an overall increase of fifty times as you go from 0.5 ha of land per person to 0.125 ha of land per person.

This can best be illustrated by two hypothetical numerical examples. Suppose the total amount of agricultural land available in a particular region per person is 2 ha (the amount of agricultural land available per person in the United States). Assume that a person living in this region wants to eat a diet of 12 MJ food energy per day entirely of vegetable products; he can get it by putting into crop production less than 1 GJ/person/yr of fossil fuel energy. If, however, he decides that he would like a U.S.-type diet, which is about 8 MJ/day of animal, bird, and fish products (including eggs and milk) and 4 MJ/day of vegetable products, he can still get it by putting less than 1 GJ/person/yr of fossil fuel energy into crop and animal production, assuming he uses half his land for crops and half for animals.

If, however, he lives in a region in which the total amount of agricultural land available is only 0.2 ha per person (which is about the amount of agricultural land available per person in West Germany), he would have to put about 2.5 GJ/person/yr of fossil fuel energy into crop production to give a diet of 12 MJ/day entirely of vegetable products. If, however, he too wants a U.S.-type diet of 8 MJ/day of animal products and 4 MJ/day of vegetable products, and if he decided to devote half his land to crops and half to animals, he would have to put in about 1.5 GJ/person/yr into crop production but 45 GJ/person/yr into animal production—a total of 46.5 GJ/person/yr. (The United States puts 10.8 GJ/person/yr into total crop and animal production.)

It would be rash to jump to the conclusion that the world food problem in relation to fossil fuel energy usage could be solved by everybody living entirely on a diet of vegetable products. In the whole world there is about twice as much grassland as arable land. (By grassland is meant land which is unsuitable for growing crops, even if it was or could be ploughed up and cultivated.) Grassland can support animals; if it is not used for this purpose it cannot contribute anything to world food supplies. Provided that animals can live entirely off this land by grazing and by cutting the grass and converting it into silage for those periods when grazing is not available, this is an excellent thing to do with such land. The energy output:input ratio for range-fed beef in the United States is about 2. It is only when animals are reared intensively and arable land has to be used to grow crops to feed them that animal production becomes highly fossil fuel energy-demanding because animals are such poor converters of energy, so that feedlot beef in the United States has an energy output:input ratio of only 0.1.

The very poor way in which we manage to use the abundant energy of the sun at present is illustrated by the work of Love (1970), showing that even range-fed beef in the western United States produces only 0.8 GJ/ha of meat for a solar energy input of 30,000 GJ/ha. MacFadyen (1964) showed that bullocks in the United Kingdom fed entirely on grass, produce only 1.25 GJ/ha of food energy, and use 200 GJ/ha of grass energy to do so, which requires 20,000 GJ/ha of solar energy to produce it. The only reason why this type of animal production does not require a lot of fossil fuel energy is that there is sufficient land available. Also, animal production is not only energy-demanding, it is labor-demanding, as the average output per man-hour for crop production in the United States is 3,000 MJ but for animal production is only about 100 MJ.

Further, even if the world decided to live entirely on a vegetable diet there are limits to the extent to which crop yields per ha can be increased by injecting fossil fuel energy. In the United States, the best yields of energy from crops are about 80 GJ/ha, which is about half the total yield which is the theoretically possible photosynthetic capability of the plants—with photosynthesis as it is at present and not improved by some of the methods possible.

In order to relate the information in figures 14 and 15 to the real world situation, it is necessary to know how much arable land and how much grassland are available per head of population in all the regions of the world. This information is given for the major countries in table 37 and summarized for the world as a whole in table 38.

Table 37. World Population and Land, 1977

Country	Population millions	Arable land per person (ha)	Grassland per person (ha)	Total per person (ha)
USSR	261	0.88	1.40	2.28
Burma	24	0.61	. .	0.61
Cambodia	6	0.46	. .	0.46
Sri Lanka	12	0.13	0.01	0.14
India	548	0.30	0.03	0.33
Indonesia	110	0.16	. .	0.16
Pakistan	95	0.27	. .	0.27
Malaysia	9	0.29	. .	0.29
Thailand	29	0.35	. .	0.35
Philippines	30	0.37	. .	0.37
China	875	0.12	0.20	0.32
North Vietnam	17	0.08	. .	0.08
South Vietnam	16	0.20	0.19	0.39
North Korea	10	0.08	. .	0.08
South Korea	27	0.08	. .	0 08
United Arab Republic	38	0.07	. .	0.07
Austria	8	0.20	0.27	0.47
Belgium	11	0.08	0.07	0.15
Bulgaria	10	0.47	0.12	0.59
Czechoslovakia	17	0.32	0.11	0.43
Finland	5	0.49	0.02	0.51
France	57	0.37	0.23	0.60
East Germany	22	0.23	0.06	0.29
West Germany	66	0.13	0.09	0.22
Hungary	12	0.45	0.11	0.56
Ireland	3	0.36	0.91	1.27
Italy	62	0.25	0.08	0.33
Netherlands	14	0.07	0.09	0.16
Poland	37	0.43	0.11	0.54
United Kingdom	57	0.13	0.22	0.35
Yugoslavia	23	0.36	0.27	0.63

Country	Population millions	Arable land per person (ha)	Grassland per person (ha)	Total per person (ha)
United States	220	0.84	1.16	2.0
Canada	23	1.80	0.93	2.7
Mexico	43	0.46	1.70	2.2
Argentina	26	1.10	4.30	5.4
Brazil	75	0.25	1.40	1.7
Columbia	18	0.28	0.81	1.1
Peru	13	0.14	1.40	1.5
Uruguay	4	0.61	3.70	4.3
Venezuela	8	0.33	2.20	2.5
Paraguay	2	0.48	5.70	6.2
Bolivia	3	0.80	2.90	3.7
Australia	13	2.60	35.00	37.6
New Zealand	3	0.25	4.30	4.6
Algeria	12	0.57	3.10	3.7
Central African Republic	2	3.60	0.02	3.6
Chad	4	2.30	13.00	15.3
Congo	19	2.60	0.13	2.7
Ethiopia	25	0.46	2.70	3.2
Ghana	8	0.63	. .	0.6
Kenya	8	0.21	0.48	0.7
Liberia	3	0.76	0.09	0.8
Madagascar	7	0.41	3.30	3.7
Morocco	12	0.63	0.62	1.3
Nigeria	44	0.50	. .	0.5
South Africa	16	0.76	5.70	6.5
Sudan	13	0.56	1.90	2.5
Tanzania	11	0.83	2.90	3.7

Source: FAO statistics.

Table 38. World Population (in Millions)
and Land (in Hectares), 1977

	More-developed regions*	Less-developed regions*
Population	1000	3000
Arable land	687 million	741 million
Grassland	1319 million	1536 million
Arable and grassland (agricultural land)	2006 million	2277 million
Arable land per person	0.69	0.25
Grassland per person	1.32	0.51
Agricultural land per person	2.00	0.76

Source: FAO statistics.
*This is a very arbitrary classification. There are rich and poor in all countries —this is the significant distinction that decides whether an individual is under-nourished or not, not where he lives. Also, some nations are well developed in some regions and poorly developed in others. However, the table gives a broad picture of the correct order and illustrates that, even within the bounds of considerable error, there is a significant difference between the developed countries and the Third World in pressure of population on land.

It will be seen that many countries in the world, including many of the highly industrialized nations of Europe as well as many of the nations of the Third World, have levels of land per person which are low enough to make very high demands for fossil fuel energy in order to nourish their population, and are in a region where these energy demands will escalate very rapidly as populations increase.

For example, the United Kingdom has 0.22 ha/person of grassland and 0.13 ha/person of arable land. From the grassland, according to figures 14 and 15, it should be able to produce 13.2 GJ/ha/yr of animal products, enough for 8 MJ per day for each of its population, by putting in about

5 GJ/person/yr of fossil fuel energy, and, from the arable land, 11.5 GJ/ha/yr of vegetable products, enough for 4 MJ per day for each of its population, but an input of about 1 GJ/person/yr. That is, the whole population could be fed by using a total of 6 GJ/person/yr of fossil fuel energy in the total U.K. system of agricultural production. In fact, 7.1 GJ/person/yr are put into this system, but enough food for only half the population is actually produced.

India has only 0.03 ha/person of grassland but 0.33 ha/person of arable land. If all the land were used for crop production, 12 MJ/day vegetable food could be produced for all the population by an input of 1.4 GJ/person/yr of fossil fuel energy. However, if half the land were used for animals and only half for crops, the fossil fuel energy input required for 8 MJ/day of animal products and 4 MJ/day of vegetable products would be 10.8 GJ/person/yr, as much as the United States now uses for primary agricultural production.

For the world as a whole, from the figures in table 38, the grasslands of the more developed countries could supply 2.2 GJ/ha/yr of animal products (8 MJ/day/person) for a fossil fuel energy input of 0.2 GJ/person/yr and the arable land could supply 2.2 GJ/ha/yr of vegetable products (4 MJ/day/person) for another 0.2 GJ/person/yr. The less-developed countries could get 5.7 GJ/ha/yr of animal products (8 MJ/day/person) from their grassland for a fossil fuel energy input of 0.18 GJ/person/yr and 6 GJ/ha/yr (4 MJ/day/person) from their arable land for an input of 0.4 GJ/person/yr.

At present the United States is not under great pressure because it is well off for land. It produces enough food to feed its own population of 220 million and to provide a surplus which, if it could all be processed, transported, and distributed without any loss, would be sufficient to feed a further 150 million people. It could thus support a population of 370 million if it exported no agricultural produce. If it had such a population, the amount of arable land available per person would be 0.50 ha and the amount of grassland available per person would be 0.69 ha. According to figures 14 and 15, with this amount of land the grassland should be able to produce 4.3 GJ/ha/yr of animal products, enough for 8 MJ/day for 370 million people for an input of about 0.4 GJ/person/yr of fossil fuel energy, and the arable land should be able to produce 3.0 GJ/ha/yr of vegetable products, enough for 4 MJ/day for 370 million people for an input of about 0.2 GJ/person/yr of fossil fuel energy. That is, 370 million people could be supplied with a present U.S.-type diet by using a total of 0.6 GJ/person/yr in the total U.S. system of primary agricultural production. Actually this system uses 10.8 GJ/person/yr for a population of 220 million, which is equivalent to 6.4 GJ/person/yr for a population of 370 million.

The information in figures 14 and 15 shows the minimum amounts of fossil fuel energy inputs which are needed to produce the required food energy outputs, assuming that the most energy-efficient systems of crop and animal production are selected. This does not imply that everybody has to live on a diet of corn. Mellanby's suggestions with regard to agricultural production in the United Kingdom indicate that the agricultural system of the United States, the U.K., and probably of all other countries in the world are a very long way from optimization as far as energy usage is concerned.

Still, it should be remembered that despite the apparent implication that much more fossil fuel energy is used in primary agricultural production in the United States than is really needed to produce the present output of food, the total amount used for this purpose is only 3.1 percent of the total fossil fuel energy used by the nation. It is not primary production of crops and animals which is the real culprit. One of the best things we *can* do with oil is to eat it, certainly a much better way to use it than many of the other ways in which it is used. The answer to the question, How long can we go on eating oil? is: For a very long time, provided that we use it as efficiently as possible in primary agricultural production and cut down drastically on the other uses we make of it. Nevertheless, however economical we may be, the world's limited and irreplaceable supplies of fossil fuel will eventually give out. If we are careful and sensible, we can buy enough time to discover and develop other technologies of food production which are not dependent on fossil fuel but which use the abundant and lasting energy of the sun. But not if we squander oil at the rate which we are doing at present.

It is pertinent to ask whether in view of the apparently unnecessarily high input of fossil fuel energy into U.S. agriculture, U.S. farming is more productive than that of other countries both with respect to yields per ha and to outputs per man-hour—that is, whether injection of energy enables better use to be made of both land and man.

Where crops are grown intensively, for instance, corn and rice, outputs per ha of metabolically utilizable food energy are somewhat better in the United States than are gained from intensively grown crops in smaller developed countries such as the United Kingdom. For example, in the United States from 1970 to 1974 corn gave, on the average, 76.9 GJ/ha/yr and rice gave, on the average 84.1 GJ/ha/yr. In the United Kingdom from 1970 to 1974 wheat gave 56.2 GJ/ha/yr and potatoes gave 56.9 GJ/ha/yr. By contrast, rice production in a Third World peasant community gave only 22.9 GJ/ha/yr, corn gave only 15.1 GJ/ha/yr, and wheat gave only 11.2 GJ/ha/yr. So in intensive cultivation of crops, the United States does a great deal better that the Third World peasant but not as much better than the United Kingdom as would be expected from a comparison of the energy injected per ha and the amount of land per person in each of the two countries. (The United States uses about 30 GJ/ha of fossil fuel to grow corn, about 65 GJ/ha to grow rice, and has about 0.55 ha of cropland per person. The United Kingdom uses about 18 GJ/ha of fossil fuel to grow wheat and about 36 GJ/ha to grow potatoes and has only about 0.08 ha of cropland per person.)

However, where crops in the United States are not grown intensively, the yields per ha are lower than those in the United Kingdom, which has to get the maximum yield it can from the cropland available whereas in the United States, with more cropland available, it may be more economical to the farmer to plant another ha rather than to apply more fertilizer. So average yields from nonintensive wheat in the United States are about 28 GJ/ha/yr compared with about 56 GJ/ha/yr for wheat in the United Kingdom. This tendency to use more land rather than to put in energy, which is a feasible practice only in countries such as the United States which have relatively large amounts of cropland per person (at present!), ought to reduce the amounts of energy used per person and per ha for primary crop production in the United States compared with the United Kingdom. Although is does reduce the amount per ha it does not seem to reduce the amount per person (U.S. primary crop production, energy input to cropland, is 12.9 GJ/ha/yr and 7.6 GJ/person/yr; U.K. primary crop production, energy input to cropland, is 49.4 GJ/ha/yr and 4.3

GJ/person/yr.) The reason for this discrepancy is that the United States produces enough food for 370 million people whereas the United Kingdom produces enough for only 25 million people. If the figures are adjusted on this basis they become 4.5 GJ/person/yr for the United States and 9.4 GJ/person/yr for the United Kingdom.

As far as food energy output per man-hour is concerned, intensive crop production in both the United States and United Kingdom give roughly equal values. Thus corn in the United States gives 3,800 MJ/man-hour, rice in the United States gives 2,800 MJ/man-hour, and wheat in the United Kingdom gives 3,040 MJ/man-hour. In contrast, a Third World peasant village obtains only about 33 MJ/man-hour from corn and 40 MJ/man-hour from rice. So, on the face of it, the developed countries score over the Third World by putting fossil fuel energy into their primary crop production and getting not only about four to five times greater food energy yields per ha but about 100 times bigger food energy outputs per man-hour.

However, this calculation may conceal the real truth. The U.S. agricultural worker feeds himself and sixty other people and uses only 3.1 percent of the total energy used by the nation to do it. But 13.8 percent of the total energy used by the nation is used in the postfarm food system and a great many more people are employed in it than are employed on farms. It is estimated that there are about 20 million people in the United States working a total of about 40 billion man-hours in various parts of the food systems including production, processing, distribution, and any other food-related work, and that the total food energy produced by the U.S. food system is about 2,000 MGJ. Thus the output per man-hour for the U.S. food system as a whole is about 50 MJ/man-hour—not much different from the 40

MJ/man-hour achieved by the Third World villages, despite all the chemical and mechanical aids and all the fossil fuel energy which the U.S. worker in any part of the food system has at his disposal.

So, what the United States achieves by putting into its total food system 16.9 percent of the total fossil fuel energy used by the nation, or 5.6 percent of the total fossil fuel energy currently produced in the whole world, is four to five times as much yield of food energy per ha than a Third World peasant village but no better output per man-hour. (The picture in the United Kingdom is, according to Leach, very similar: about 4 million workers in the U.K. food system working a total of 8 billion man-hours to give 261 MGJ of food energy equivalent to about 30-35 MJ/man-hour.)

None of these comparisons between the U.S. and the Third World village take any account of labor spent on food preparation. Does the U.S. homemaker with a kitchen full of appliances powered by fossil fuel energy and all the convenience and ready-prepared foods available from the supermarket spend a great deal less energy on food preparation than a counterpart in the Third World? Almost certainly, although perhaps not to the extent one might think. Vanek (1974) showed that for U.S. women who did not have full-time jobs outside the home, average weekly hours spent on food preparation fell only from twenty-three to eighteen from 1926 to 1968 while average weekly hours spent on shopping rose from four to eight hours a week. However, this survey did not include women with full-time jobs so is probably misleading. Even if input of fossil fuel energy into the U.S. food system has not improved the output of food energy per man-hour over that in a Third World village, it has almost certainly very substantially increased the output per woman-hour.

I am a citizen of the United Kingdom, not of the United States. Nevertheless, I have a deep love and concern for the American people as well as for the people of my own country and all the people in the world. The people of the United States have achieved so much and have so much potential that it would be appalling if they were to lose it all. But, when I consider the social ability that has created a united nation in only about a hundred years following a divisive civil war and an influx of peoples of all types of racial and ethnic origins; when I consider the economic ability that has enabled them in such a short time to build up the wealthiest society and one of the highest standards of living in the world; when I consider the scientific and technological skills that have made this possible by invention and innovation and have created in so few years the great industrial and productive capacity of the nation; when I consider the moral strength that has been the driving force (even if nowadays that moral strength sometimes seems obscured, I believe it is still there)—when I consider all these things, I believe that the U.S. people have the capability of solving the social, economic, and technological problems of ensuring that their descendants are adequately fed, and of making a substantial contribution to solving the problems of feeding the world, just as I believe that the people of my own country and other developed countries also have that capability, though they may be limited in what they could do by the fact that their resources and wealth are less than those of the United States.

But potential and capability are effective only if they are translated into action, and this requires the vision, will, understanding, and unselfishness to do it. The writing is on the wall and none of the developed countries can afford to ignore it. It would be disastrous if the people of the

United States were complacent enough to believe that their
wealth and power could protect them forever from the
consequences of eating oil. The warning implicit in Shelley's
poem should be heeded as a spur to action:

> I met a traveller from an antique land
> Who said: "Two vast and trunkless legs of stone
> Stand in the desert. Near them on the sand,
> Half sunk, a shattered visage lies
> And on the pedestal these words appear:
> 'My name is Ozymandias, king of kings;
> Look on my works, ye mighty, and despair!'.
> Nothing besides remains. Round the decay
> Of that colossal wreck, boundless and bare,
> The lone and level sands stretch far away.

Epilogue

There is no world shortage of energy, only a shortage of knowledge of how to use it. In the United States the sun pours down an average of 140 GJ/ha/day—the equivalent of about 1,000 U.S. gal of oil on every ha every day.

Even if the best fast breeder reactor technology, with all its attendant risks and hazards, using all probable sources of uranium in the world, could be developed, it would provide for the world a total of about 300 million MGJ—about 1/10 of the total solar energy which falls on the world every year. It must be remembered that uranium is also an irreplaceable and limited fossil fuel resource.

The scientific and engineering ingenuity that has sent men to the moon; developed complex weapons; produced the drugs, pesticides, plastics, synthetic fibers, and the myriad of other products of chemical industry; and built skyscrapers, bridges, and all the other marvels of engineering, should, if diverted to the purpose, be able to solve the problem of harnessing the unlimited energy of the sun and to do what nature does even in its simplest photosynthesizing organism.

The scientists of the world might well, with humility, pray:

> We ask you, Lord, on bended knees
> To grant us knowledge, if you please,
> Of processes which match in skill
> The use plants make of chlorophyll.

Appendix

Table 1. Solar Energy

| | Whole world | Total average solar energy falling on: | | | |
		U.S. (total)	U.S. (sunnier parts)	U.K.	Tropical (deserts)
Yearly	3 billion MGJ/yr*	50 million MGJ/yr		0.88 million MGJ/yr	
Daily		140 GJ/ ha/day	200 GJ/ ha/day	100 GJ/ ha/day	300 GJ/ ha/day

*Compare with possible total world resources of fossil fuels (85.3 million MGJ) or possible total world resources of atomic energy, even using fast breeder reactors (292 million MGJ).

Table 2. World Energy Resources, 1977

	Proved million MGJ	Possible million MGJ	1972 consumed thousand MGJ
Coal and lignite	12.7	70.0	80
Oil	2.6	9.2	103
Natural gas	2.3	6.1	45
Total	17.6	85.3	238

Note: Uranium, in thermal reactors, 2.2 million MGJ proved, 4.9 million MGJ possible. In fast breeder reactors, 188 million MGJ proved, 292 million MGJ possible.

Table 3. Population (in Millions) and Land (in Hectares), 1977

	U.S.	U.K.	India*
Total population	220	57	548
Total land area	919 million	24 million	326 million
Total grassland	256 million	12.3 million	14 million
Total arable land	185 million	7.4 million	162 million
Total cropland included in arable	*120 million*	*4.8 million*	*105 million*
Total arable and grassland (agricultural land)	441 million	19.7 million	176 million
Grassland per person	1.16	0.22	0.03
Arable land per person	0.84	0.13	0.30
Agricultural land per person	2.00	0.35	0.33
Cropland per person	*0.55*	*0.08*	*0.19*

*The figures for India are very approximate because no reliable sources of information have been located by the author.

Table 4. Energy and Food Production, 1970

	U.S.	U.K.	India*
Total fossil fuel energy (MGJ/yr) put into:			
Primary crop production	1543	227	100
Primary agricultural production	2204	396	100
Total food system	9842	1965	?
Total nation for all purposes	71320	8618	?
Fossil fuel energy (GJ/yr) put into:			
Primary crop production	7.6	4.1	0.2
Primary agricultural production	10.8	7.1	0.2
Total food system	48.2	35.2	?
Total nation for all purposes	349	154	?
Fossil fuel energy per ha (GJ/yr) put into:			
Primary crop production (cropland only)	12.9	47.2	1.0
Primary agricultural production (total agricultural land)	5.0	20.0	0.6
Total food energy (MGJ/yr):			
Produced at farm gate	1911	135	?
Wasted in processing and distribution	191	13	?
Supplied to consumers	1720†	122	?
Eaten or wasted by total population	973†	276	1700
Eaten or wasted per person	13.07	13.27	8.5

Note: The minimum daily intake to preserve health is 8 MJ/day. Recommended adequate daily intake is 12 MJ/day.

*The figures for India are very approximate because no reliable sources of information have been located by the author.

†From these figures it appears that the United States has 747 MGJ/yr of food energy available for export or enough to give 170 million people 12 MJ/day if none were lost in processing, transport, or distribution.

References and Further Reading

The author acknowledges with gratitude the following as sources of information for this book. The book by Leach, *Energy and Food Production,* is particularly informative on the U.K. food system. Most of the books and papers below contain copious additional references that will be as informative to the reader who wishes to study the subject further as they have been to the author.

References

Adelson, S. F. 1961. *J. Amer. Dietetic Asscn.* 39:578; 1963. *J. Home Economics.* 55:8.

Blaxter, K. L. 1975. *J. Sci. Fd. Agric.* 26:1055.

Bleasdale, J. K. A. 1976. *Chem. and Ind.* No. 13, p. 553.

Chapman, P. 1975. Energy Analysis Group, Open University, Report ERG006. United Kingdom: Milton Keynes.

Ennis, W. B. 1970. *Technological Economics of Crop Protection.* Monograph no. 36. Society of Chemical Industry: London.

Ennis, W. B.; Jansen, L. L. ; Ellis, I. T.; and Newsom, L. D. 1967. *The World Food Problem.* Vol. 3. Washington.

Fears, R. 1976. *New Scientist.* 69:606.

Green, M. B. 1976. "Energy in Agriculture." *Chem. and Ind.* No. 15, p. 641.

Green, M. B., and McCulloch, A. 1976. *J. Sci. Fd. Agric.* 27: 95.

Harrison, G. G. 1975. *J. Nutrition Education.* 7:1.

Hawthorn, J. 1975. *Span.* 18:15.

Hill, L. D., and Erickson, S. 1976. *Ag. World.* 2:1.

Imperial Chemical Industries, Agricultural Division. 1974. "The Energy Input to a Bag of Fertilizer." Billingham, England.

Kling, W. 1943. *J. Farm Economics.* 25:848.

Leach, G. 1976. *Energy and Food Production.* Guildford, England: IPC Science and Technology Press.

Lee, R. B. 1969. "Kung Bushmen Subsistence." In *Environmental and Cultural Behaviour,* ed. A. P. Vayda. New York: Natural History Press.

Love, R. M. 1970. *Scientific American.* 222:88.

MacFadyen, A. 1964. *Grazing in Terrestrial Environments.* Oxford, England: Blackwell.

Makhijani, A. 1975. *Energy and Agriculture in the Third World.* Cambridge, Mass.: Ballinger Publishing Co.

Mellanby, K. 1975. "Can Britain Feed Itself?" London: Merlin Press, 3 January 1975. *London Times.*

Ministry of Agriculture, Fisheries and Food, United Kingdom. 1973. Technical Bulletin no. 32, p. 355. London.

Prassad, C. R. 1974. *Economic and Political Weekly.* 9:1347.

Preston, R. 1974. Commission Nacional de la Industria Azucarera. Mexico City.

Price Jones, D. Personal communication.

Reid, D. 1970. *J. Agric. Sci. Camb.* 74:227.

Revelle, R. 1976. *Scientific American.* 235:164.

Rice, R. A. 1972. *Technol. Rev.* 75:32.

Rook, J. A. S. 1976. *Chem. and Ind.* No. 14, p. 581.

Roy, R. 1976. "Wastage in the U.K. Food System." Earth Resources Research. London.

Slesser, M. 1973. *J. Sci. Fd. Agric.* 24:1193.

Steinhart. J. S., and Steinhart, C. E. 1974. *Science.* 184:307.

Stigler, G. 1945. *J. Farm Economics.* 27:2.

Taylor, T. B., and Humpstone, G. C. 1973. *The Restoration of the Earth.* New York: Harper & Row.

Tudge, C. 1975. *New Scientist.* 66:138.

United Nations. 1968. "International Action To Avert the Impending Protein Crisis." New York.

United States Department of Agriculture. 1965. "Losses in Agriculture." Washington.

Vanek, J. 1974. *Scientific American.* 231:116.

Further Reading

A Time to Choose: America's Energy Future. 1974. Cambridge, Mass.: Ballinger Publishing Co.

Barrons, K. C. 1973. *The Food in Your Future.* New York: Van Nostrand Reinhold Co.

Black, J. H. 1971. *Ann. App. Biol.* 67:272.

Chemical Society. 1976. *Conservation of Resources.* Special Publication No. 27. London.

Hall, D. O. 1974. International Solar Energy Society. London.

Hirst, E. 1974. *Science.* 184:134.

Ministry of Agriculture, Fisheries and Food, United Kingdom. 1974. *Report of the Energy Working Party.* London.

Organisation for Economic Co-operation and Development. 1967. "The Food Problem of Developing Countries." Paris.

Pimental, D. 1973. *Science.* 182:43.

Search. 7:10. 1976. Sydney, Australia.

Index